FRED PERRY | BRITISH TENNIS LEGEND

KEVIN JEFFERYS

First published by Pitch Publishing, 2017

Pitch Publishing
A2 Yeoman Gate
Yeoman Way
Worthing
Sussex
BN13 3QZ

www.pitchpublishing.co.uk
info@pitchpublishing.co.uk

A CIP catalogue record is available for this book
from the British Library.

ISBN 978-1-78531-290-8

Contents

To my family, with love and thanks

Preface and Acknowledgements

THE realisation that I would never be able to master the art of playing the game anything like Fred Perry came quite early on in my tennis career (using the word 'career' in the loosest possible sense).

As a teenager in the 1970s, I spent several happy summers travelling around my local area and competing in some of the numerous weekly tournaments held during the school holidays. My finest hour in singles appeared to have arrived in 1976 when – aided by withdrawals among several players affected by the blistering heat of that summer – at one such event I reached the semi-finals of the boys' singles.

As the match unfolded I surprised myself by taking the first set and storming to a 5-1 lead in the second, leaving me just one game away from victory and a place in the final. Until this point my opponent, the annoyingly tall, dark and handsome number one seed, had spent most of his time glancing across and smiling at his entourage of mostly female court-side followers. At this 11th hour, however, he decided it was time to rouse himself. Spraying winners to all parts of the court, he pulled back to take the second set 7-5 and proceeded to win the match easily in the third.

My singles ambitions thwarted, I decided that doubles was the thing for me, and throughout my adult life I've been fortunate to derive years of great pleasure and enjoyment from club doubles. But as a lifelong tennis fan I've always retained a fascination with the individual greats of the sport, from the Borgs and McEnroes of my youth to the Federers and Murrays of today, trying to watch and understand what it is that makes the top players really tick. Hence it's been a real pleasure for me to research and write about one of the true legends of modern lawn tennis and of British sport more generally.

This is Fred Perry's story.

* * *

I am grateful to the librarians and archivists at various institutions for facilitating access to important collections of material relating to Perry's career, notably to the staff of the Wimbledon Library at the All England Club. My debt to the writings and recollections of former players, journalists and observers of the tennis scene is suitably acknowledged, I hope, in the Notes at the end of the book.

For permission to use the photographs reproduced in the book I'd like to thank Press Association Images, and in particular Sam Harrison. The front cover jacket shows Perry in action during his second Wimbledon final, July 1935. On the back cover, Perry is seen holding the trophy after his third victory in the US Championships, September 1936. Images courtesy of Getty Images. I'm also grateful to Kate for helping in the preparation of the manuscript; to Graham Hales for assistance with the photos; to Duncan Olner for the cover design; and to Jane and Paul Camillin at Pitch Publishing for their support and encouragement in bringing the project to fruition. While grateful to all those concerned for their valuable help and guidance, it should be added that responsibility for any errors or omissions rests with me alone.

Kevin Jefferys, April 2017

Introduction: 'Perry is not a popular champion at home'

ALL looked set fair on the afternoon of Friday 6 July 1934 for a famous British sporting triumph. In front of the packed stands on Wimbledon's Centre Court, Fred Perry played some dazzling tennis in his attempt to become the first home player to take the men's singles title since 1909.

Although his Australian opponent, the defending champion Jack Crawford, took an early lead in the opening set, Perry entered into what the later American Wimbledon winner Arthur Ashe described as one of those 'serene highs' that tennis players occasionally experience: a period of sustained, almost unplayable brilliance.

The Englishman claimed 12 games in succession as his virtually error-free serving, volleying and ground strokes swept him to a 6-3, 6-0 advantage; Crawford managed just a meagre eight points in the second set. The third set was closer, but after little more than an hour's play Perry was victorious. He did a cartwheel to celebrate his straight-sets win, followed by a trademark leap over the net to shake his opponent's hand.

Even in the pre-television age, there were plenty of court-side photographers on hand to ensure that newspaper images of the athletic young champion would be recognisable around the world.

The American Jack Kramer, another post-war Wimbledon winner, wrote in his memoirs about the glamour associated with the sport when he was growing up in the 1930s, 'If you never saw tennis players in their long white flannels, I cannot begin to explain to you how majestic they appeared.'

With film-star good looks and slicked-back hair, the imposing young Englishman illustrated Kramer's point more than most. 'Fred Perry in a linen shirt, matching pants, everything tailored: there was never a champion in any sport who looked more like a champion than Fred Perry.'[1]

Yet beneath the surface, something was amiss on that warm July afternoon. In part this was because the last point of the contest was an anti-climax; Crawford's reign as champion ended with the indignity of serving a double fault. Fred Burrow, the referee of the tournament, reflected that this 'had the unfortunate effect of depriving the winner of a great deal of the applause he most certainly ought to have received... The stands were too stupefied at the sudden and unfortunate finish to give Perry... a proper tribute'.[2]

But the muted response of the 15,000-strong crowd was not simply the result of a tame finish to the match. Centre Court spectators were not always averse to greeting new champions with gusto. Twenty-four hours after Perry's win, Worcestershire's Dorothy Round made it a British double by winning a thrilling women's final. According to one close observer of the tennis scene, Teddy Tinling, who was present on both days, 'The crowd were roused to a far greater pitch of excitement than that which had greeted Perry's victory.' There were 'deafening cheers' from all sides, said Tinling, and even King George V and Queen Mary, attending to support Miss Round, 'seemed quite overwhelmed'.[3]

The reality was that many of the onlookers were underwhelmed by what they witnessed on 6 July. Throughout the Perry–Crawford encounter, not simply at the end, the atmosphere was subdued. 'For a Wimbledon final,' noted the match report in *The Times*, 'there was a strange lack of excitement in the crowded galleries.'[4] What the role of the crowd during and at the end of the match implied was that, in spite of his striking physical appearance and his claim to have become the best player in the world, there was little instinctive rapport between Perry and his audience.

Remarkably, in view of the long years since 1909 without British men's success at Wimbledon, there appeared to be warmer support for the vanquished than the victor. According to a reporter from the Associated Press, Crawford received greater applause for his endeavours than Perry.

Confirmation that more was at work than British sympathy for a gallant loser came a week later. In its review of the tournament the official mouthpiece of the game's governing body in Britain, the Lawn Tennis Association (LTA), described Perry's win as the finest individual achievement by an Englishman since the Great War. But it also adopted an unmistakably jarring tone, 'Frankly many of us had not believed that Perry had such tennis in him... In spite of his defeat much of the honours of the 1934 Championship Meeting must go to J. H. Crawford.'[5]

The new champion would not have been surprised by this account, for within half an hour of coming off court after the final he experienced at first hand the frostiness of some sections of the British tennis establishment towards his victory. In the days of unpaid amateur competition, when the reward for winning Wimbledon was not a sizeable cheque but a replica trophy, a medal, a shopping voucher valued at £25 and a gold laurel wreath embroidered on a silk ribbon, there were no on-court presentation ceremonies. Instead it was the custom to offer congratulations in the changing rooms.

Perry was greeted by family and friends coming off court, but as he settled into the bath to soak and recover from his exertions, he overheard a Wimbledon committee member, Brame Hillyard, offering congratulations to Jack Crawford and saying, 'This was one day when the best man didn't win.'

It was an incident that still rankled with Perry when he published his autobiography 50 years later. He couldn't believe his ears, he recalled, adding that he immediately jumped out of the bath to find that Crawford had been given a bottle of champagne. The traditional tie, also offered to Wimbledon champions to signify membership of the prestigious All England Club (AEC), was left unceremoniously on the back of a chair for Perry to collect. 'I don't think I've ever been so angry in my life,' he wrote. 'Instead of Fred J. Perry the champ, I felt like Fred J. Muggs the chimp. The Perry balloon was certainly deflated.'[6]

It may have been the case that Perry embellished, or according to some possibly even fabricated, the oft-repeated story of what was said in the dressing rooms; a few instances of faulty memory in his 1984 memoirs have recently been highlighted.[7]

At the time, the new champion certainly perked up sufficiently to enjoy evening and overnight celebrations following his victory, including dinner at the Savoy hotel in London before hitting the party trail. Almost without sleep, he returned to Wimbledon the following day, where he and Dorothy Round – following her singles victory – were presented to the King and Queen. But in spite of the cheers that accompanied the two champions as they made their way to the royal box, there was no doubt that winning Wimbledon was a bittersweet experience for Perry. It took several days, and a threat not to represent his country in a forthcoming international tie, for him to receive an apology for what transpired in the dressing room after the men's final. In spite of the smiles to camera and the handshakes of congratulation, it was obvious that tensions lingered.

What, then, was the explanation for Perry's ambivalent relationship with the Wimbledon crowds and the British tennis authorities? A large body of evidence (to be outlined in the following chapters) points to a protracted and complex tale of mutual mistrust. Although Perry may have exaggerated certain details in his later reflections, the thrust of his argument, and his enduring sense of grievance about how he was treated by the powers-that-be, was strikingly clear-cut.

In his 1984 memoirs Perry summed up his side of the story by citing an American writer, John R. Tunis, who observed in a 1934 article for *Esquire* magazine that 'Wimbledon is the most snobbish centre of sport in the world'. The members of the All-England Club, it was claimed, seemed resentful that the revival of British men's tennis after a long period in the doldrums had been spearheaded by a player without a traditional public school, university-educated background. The uncomfortable truth, according to John Tunis, was that despite his great triumph, 'Perry is not a popular champion at home.'[8]

* * *

Fred Perry went on to achieve considerable fame and – later on in his life – fortune. His Wimbledon victory in 1934 was the first of three successive triumphs in London SW19, and until the end of 1936 he remained the undisputed world number one in the amateur game. In addition to Wimbledon, he won the national championships of Australia, France and (on three occasions) the United States, making him the first player to claim all four 'grand slam' titles, though not in the same calendar year: that honour was taken by Donald Budge in 1938.

As well as eight major singles titles, like many other top players of his era he played tournament doubles to keep himself sharp, and he won the French and Australian men's titles as well as claiming four mixed doubles triumphs – a combined total of 14 top-level successes. He also played the lead role in Britain's domination of the premier international competition in tennis, the Davis Cup, which was won on four successive occasions between 1933 and 1936. And after he left amateur tennis, he additionally claimed two prestigious US Pro titles, in 1938 and 1941.

All in all, Perry's record was remarkable. Only in the very recent past, with the rise of Andy Murray to world number one, has a British man come close to matching – some would say exceeding, in view of the depth of opposition and ferocity of men's tennis today – the scale of Perry's achievements. The long wait for another home-grown male winner at Wimbledon lasted for 77 years, until 2013 witnessed the first of two triumphs for Murray (who at the time of writing has a total of three grand slam titles to his name). As for the national team, it was even longer, in 2015, before Britain – inspired by the performances of Murray and his brother Jamie – once again claimed the Davis Cup. Fifty years on from the 1934 Wimbledon final, in a survey of 2,000 people carried out by the British Market Research Bureau aimed at finding the 'Best of the Best' British sportsmen of the 20th century, it was no surprise that Perry was the only tennis player on the list. The same applied when in 2007 *Observer* journalist Jon Henderson published a book of *Sporting Heroes*, a celebration of the nation's 100 greatest sports men and women of all time.[9]

This book sets out to examine afresh the life and career of Fred Perry, and in particular to explore the issue of why – despite building up a reputation in the 1930s as one of the first modern-style global sports celebrities – acclaim for him was not readily evident among the tennis authorities in Britain, either in his prime playing days or for many years afterwards. In spite of his status as one of the best players in tennis history, only one full-length biography of Perry has so far appeared: Jon Henderson's book was published in 2009 to coincide with the hundredth anniversary of Fred's birth.[10] As a result, Perry remains understudied.

In an age when sporting biographies are plentiful, today's generation of leading players is much better served. In the case of Andy Murray, whose career is yet to be complete, several biographical accounts by journalists have already appeared, alongside three separate works of autobiographical reflections. One of the latter adopts a title – *Seventy-Seven* – that explicitly alludes to Murray at last providing a British Wimbledon winner in succession to Perry.[11]

As tennis correspondent of *The Observer*, Jon Henderson brings enormous knowledge to the subject matter of his biography and carefully outlines the main phases in Perry's playing career: his meteoric rise in the early 1930s; his capturing of eight grand slam singles titles; his role in helping Britain to win the prestigious Davis Cup on four successive occasions; and his decision to cash in on his fame by turning professional in 1936. Henderson's book is also strong in outlining what he calls Fred's 'romantic entanglements' with Hollywood actresses on his regular trips to the USA in the 1930s and in relationships which resulted in four marriages. What follows, in this new study, differs from Henderson's biography in a few key respects.

Fred Perry: British Tennis Legend, as a shorter work, focuses less on affairs of the heart and the detail of individual grand slam and Davis Cup matches (especially those in the early rounds of tournaments) and more on the social and political background that contextualises and illuminates Perry's career. In addition, by way of contrast, more attention is given here to the rights and wrongs of Perry's ongoing battles with the tennis authorities, and also to key incidents of good fortune that were crucial in facilitating his rise to the pinnacle of the world game. Three stand-out moments in particular, discussed though not emphasised in Henderson's book, will be highlighted in the chapters that follow.

British Tennis Legend also attempts, notably in the conclusion, to weigh up more fully Perry's enduring place among the greats of the sport.

The main concern of this new biography is therefore to provide a concise, up-to-date and thoroughly researched study of Britain's most successful player of the 20th century, bringing to life his strong personality – part charmer, part blunt egoist – and above all seeking to cast fresh light on why it was that, despite his record, full acceptance and recognition of Perry in the stuffy world of British tennis remained elusive for much of his life.

Simmering resentments, so evident at the time of Fred's first Wimbledon success, continued until at the end of 1936 he left the amateur game to live and work in the United States. By joining the small professional tennis circuit there, he started to earn considerable sums of money, but as a consequence was instantly banned from the world's top amateur events, including Wimbledon and the Davis Cup. In an age when professionalism was regarded as anathema by the game's governing bodies, Perry was promptly relieved of his honorary membership of the All England Club, and the tie that came with it. 'And after all the trouble they'd gone to presenting it to me,' he commented acidly in his memoirs.[12]

His troubled relationship with the powers-that-be and the manner of his exile ensured there was no enduring Perry legacy for British tennis. The LTA made little effort to build lasting success on the back of his triumphs. For many years after 1936 relations were frosty as Perry built a new life in the USA, which he found much less hidebound about social distinctions than Britain. His name remained well known throughout the world (and his bank balance healthy) following the success of the Fred Perry sportswear label, and relations with the AEC and the LTA slowly improved as the years passed with no British man to emulate his success on the world stage.

Even so, Perry was an elderly figure of 75, and pay-for-play 'open' tennis was well established, before reconciliation with the British tennis establishment was complete. The unveiling of a statue of the three-time champion at Wimbledon in 1984 was a well-intentioned and warmly appreciated gesture, but as one later obituary of Perry noted, it also drew attention to the 'embarrassing length of time' which had elapsed since Britain had a player of his capability. It had taken, as the title of an article in the leading American magazine *World Tennis* claimed, 'Fifty Years to Honor a Winner'.[13]

When he died in 1995 Perry's place as a sporting legend was beyond dispute, but for much of his life after moving to America – this book shows – he remained curiously unheralded in the land of his birth. Although highly regarded among casual followers of the sport, the hurt caused in his amateur days was not easily forgotten, either by Perry himself or by his detractors among the movers and shakers of tennis officialdom.

In order to appreciate why he was for so long the nation's unsung grand slam and Davis Cup hero, and where responsibility for this lies, we must first examine Perry's family background and the social and political world into which he grew up during and after the First World War. As we shall see, it was Fred's humble origins, together with his no-nonsense personality, that provide the key to understanding why he made as many enemies as friends in the upper- and middle-class dominated world of British tennis; why he was, in the words expressed by the American John Tunis in 1934, 'not a popular champion at home'.

1

Moving from north to south

NY CHAMPION in sport needs good fortune. In tennis, a whole host of qualities mark out those who reach the upper echelons of the game: technical mastery of a range of shots, speed around the court, stamina, a calm temperament under pressure, immense determination – all have been characteristics of the world's best players from the emergence of modern lawn tennis at the end of the 19th century through to the era of Federer, Nadal, Djokovic and Murray. But chance also plays a part.

Fred Perry believed that 15 to 20 per cent of any player's destiny was guided by luck, and at the start of his autobiography (published in 1984 with the help of *Observer* journalist Ronald Atkin) he claimed a few especially fortuitous moments helped him to build a successful career in tennis. These were his victory over the number four seed at Wimbledon in 1930, achieved in front of an LTA selection committee, which instantly awarded him a place on a British touring team overseas; reaching the final of the Davis Cup in 1931, which brought international recognition, despite Britain losing out to France; and finally winning the Davis Cup in 1933. That, he believed, was when his career 'really took off'.[1]

While these occasions were clearly key landmarks in Perry's rise to eminence, the second and third in particular owed more to his talent and determination (and that of his Davis Cup team-mates) than to pure chance. Aside from these incidents and random moments such as net cords that sometimes influence the outcome of individual matches, there were in Perry's case arguably three other crucial moments or contextual factors where providence played a vital part in his development.

Two of these three – each of which has not hitherto been adequately highlighted in discussions of Perry's career – will be discussed in later chapters. The first of them, however, came very early in his life, and was in some ways the most important, for seen in the light of his family background the prospect of Perry becoming the world's best tennis player in the mid-1930s was remote in the extreme.

Perry was a product of the industrial north of England. His father, Samuel Perry, was born in the 1870s into a working-class household in Stockport, south-east of Manchester. Today Stockport combines residential and commercial development and honours one of its most famous sons with the 'Fred Perry Way,' a 14-mile walking route around the locality, opened in 2002.

The town first expanded in the 19th century in the wake of the industrial revolution, mainly through cotton and allied industries. In the 1840s a huge viaduct was built over the River Mersey at the western edge of the town to improve railway links north and south, though some visitors were not impressed by the sight that greeted them as they arrived by train. In his famous 1840s book *The Condition of the Working Class in England*, Friedrich Engels wrote that Stockport was renowned as one of the 'duskiest, smokiest holes' in the region, and had an appearance from the viaduct that was 'excessively repellent'.[2]

Fred's grandfather, also called Samuel Perry, scraped a living by working like many of his contemporaries in the local cotton mills. Sam Perry junior was a bright child, and although opportunities for educational advancement were severely restricted for those from poor backgrounds, he won a scholarship to attend the prestigious Stockport Grammar School. His prospects were blighted when his father contracted an illness and died at an early age in the late 1880s. Instead of going to the local grammar, Sam Perry at the age of ten followed in his father's footsteps by working at the cotton factory.

Forced by his circumstances to grow up quickly, Sam began to develop an interest in trade unionism, which was well entrenched in the cotton industry. Even as a teenager, he displayed qualities that marked him out as a potential future leader within labour circles. He showed proficiency in machine drawing and construction, maths and applied mechanics, and his day-to-day work gave him a close understanding of the complex pay structures in the Lancashire cotton trade.

At the time of his 21st birthday – by which age his own son was to have played at Wimbledon – Sam was established as a pillar of the late-Victorian 'respectable' working classes. His commitment to trade unionism was reflected in his election as president of the Stockport Cotton Spinners' Association, and he devoted time away from work and study to preaching from Methodist pulpits and becoming prominent in the Manchester temperance movement.[3]

The real heart of Sam's life as a political activist was the Co-operative movement. From humble beginnings in Rochdale in the 1840s, the Co-op, with its ethos of supporting lower income families through worker ownership of industries and profit sharing, grew to become an established feature of many working-class communities. By the beginning of the 20th century, the movement had some two million members and through its various outlets had built up trade worth about £50m – nearly £4bn at today's prices. Anxious to promote Co-operative ideals, Sam was appointed as president of the Stockport Co-operative Society in 1908 and later of the Birkenhead society, two of the largest in the country.[4] By this time he also had a family to support. In 1901 he married a local girl, Hannah Birch (a fellow worker at the local cotton mill), and the couple lived in a small house at Carrington Road, Stockport.

It was in Carrington Road that two children were born, Edith in 1903 and Frederick John on 18 May 1909 (with another daughter to follow later). Just a matter of weeks after Fred's birth, the men's singles at Wimbledon, already established as the most prestigious tennis event in the world, was won for the third time by Arthur Gore, whose victory at the age of 41 made him (as he remains) the tournament's oldest singles champion. It was also to be the last time the title was captured by an Englishman for 25 years.

Edith and Fred grew up accustomed to the long absences of their father, absorbed as he was either in his work or his many improving causes. The children also found themselves frequently on the move – a recurrent theme in Fred's life – in the interest of supporting their father's burgeoning career. Fred was still very young when the family moved briefly to Bolton and then on again to Wallasey, a convenient location for Sam when he spent time during the First World War working for the Co-op in Liverpool. Fred recalled how on one occasion air raid warnings sounded suddenly at school, with the result that the children were sent into a nearby field to lie beside a large Red Cross flag in case 'the Hun' arrived imminently.[5]

As the carnage of the Great War came to a close, the Perry family found themselves on the move again. For many years Sam was a vocal advocate of direct electoral engagement to advance the Co-operative cause; this at a time when many in the movement clung to a stance of maintaining political neutrality. In 1918 agreement was finally reached to launch a fully-fledged Co-operative party, though it met with little initial success: only one of ten candidates was elected when a general election took place at the end of the year. Sam's credentials made him the natural choice to become the first secretary of the new party. This was a post he was to hold for a quarter of a century, and one that required the biggest adjustment yet for his wife and children – a move to London.

The family settled soon after the war into a solid three-bedroom house in Brentham, a new 'garden suburb' in Ealing, west London. For Sam, living at Pitshanger Lane in Ealing offered many advantages. For one thing Brentham, which became an architectural model for the likes of Hampstead garden suburb, was an example of Co-operative housing policy in practice. His end-of-terrace property was built in 1906 by Ealing Tenants Limited, which specialised in offering subsidised rents to workers who owned shares in the company.

The Brentham estate also provided the Perry family with a ready-made sense of community, notably through a well-supported local club that provided a range of social and sporting facilities. Perhaps most important, the location suited Sam's political ambitions. He was not too far from the Co-operative party's headquarters near Charing Cross station, and he was also within striking distance of the House of Commons at Westminster.

Increasingly, as he settled into London life, Sam hoped to become a Member of Parliament, making his first foray into electoral politics by standing at the Stockport by-election of 1920. He was a strong believer in close ties between the Co-op and the Labour party – 'we come of common stock; we are working for the common end', he claimed – but this strategy was not universally accepted.

The local Labour group in Stockport preferred to adopt its own candidate rather than give the Co-operative party a free run, and with left-wing votes split Perry failed to secure election both at the by-election and again when he stood for Stockport at the general election in 1922. He did though succeed in becoming MP in 1923 for Kettering, a Northants constituency with a tradition of co-operation based around the local boot and shoe industry. Unlike in Stockport, socialists and co-operators worked in harmony, and standing on a Labour-Co-operative ticket Perry won with a 2,500 majority over the Conservatives. When Labour formed its first, short-lived, government in 1924, Perry was to the fore in assisting with legislation that was close to his heart: an Act providing improved housing for the poorest sections of society.

Although it could not be known at the time, the move to London in 1919 was to be of huge significance for Fred, as well as for his father. Sam's life had been greatly influenced by a tragic event (the early death of a parent) when he was just ten years old, and Fred's future was also shaped by a major change of circumstances at the same tender age. With hindsight, it was one of the three significant pieces of good fortune, over and above those he identified in his memoirs, without which he was unlikely to have become a world-renowned star.

Tennis before the First World War was largely confined to the most affluent sections of British society, and someone like Perry, coming from humble origins in Stockport, was unlikely to have picked up a racket – still less to have competed in key tournaments and sought to build a high-profile career in the sport – if his family had not moved away from its northern working-class roots.

While the number of tennis clubs across the country was growing steadily in the early decades of the 20th century, the opportunities in the north of England were more restricted than in the London area. In the early 1920s the counties of Lancashire and Cheshire combined, covering huge tracts of land in the north-west, had fewer clubs in total than were found in Middlesex – the county Perry in due course took pride in representing.[6] In the long term, it was crucial to Fred's development that he lived not simply in the southern English heartland of lawn tennis, but in close proximity to the twin power centres of the game: the LTA, based at central London, and the All England Club at Wimbledon.

While his relationship with these bodies was to be fraught, his Ealing base provided him with openings unavailable in many other parts of the country, enabling him to come to the attention of prominent figures in the game at a relatively young age. More immediately, what the move south did was to stimulate young Fred's interest in sport. When he had time for recreation, Sam enjoyed running, bowls and in particular golf, and his liking of sport was to be taken up in full measure by his son.

Sam hoped his children would find better prospects in London than he had at a young age, and for Fred he envisaged a career in commerce or business; something which required staying on at school beyond the usual leaving age of 14. For a year or so Fred went to a local elementary school, Drayton Green, and then progressed to Ealing county school. But his heart was never in academic learning. 'I hated homework,' he later conceded. Instead he channelled his energies into a whole variety of both team and individual sports. He played for the school football and cricket teams, though he admitted to being a poor wicketkeeper. His sporting heroes were jockeys and racing-car drivers, and like so many teenage boys he dreamt of playing for one of the top soccer teams of the day such as Aston Villa.

Fred's passion for bats and balls was fuelled by the ready accessibility of excellent facilities on his doorstep. His first love was table tennis, a game he rapidly improved at by joining the local YMCA, as well as by pushing a table up against the kitchen wall in the evenings; much to the annoyance of his parents, who felt he should be doing homework. As a self-taught player, Fred held the bat with a hatchet grip rather than the conventional penholder style; in due course he transferred this grip to a tennis racket and never changed it.

Above all it was the Brentham Institute, an essential component of the garden suburb concept, which provided Perry with ample opportunities to indulge his love of games. As well as providing a venue for community meetings and dances, the club was endowed with football pitches, a cricket field, bowling greens, tennis courts and table tennis tables. This was 'paradise' after the 'bleak streets' of his early years, he claimed; for a youngster arriving from the north 'it was marvellous'.[7]

With so much on offer, Fred never really sampled tennis until he was a teenager. Many tennis clubs were restricted to adults only, and among youngsters the game was mostly confined to small numbers of private schools. It did not feature on the curriculum of Ealing school and Perry first dabbled, but no more, when he was 14. Only in the following summer, as a 15-year-old, did he start to play with any intent, a remarkably late age by modern-day standards. On a family holiday to

Eastbourne he was favourably impressed watching tennis being played at Devonshire Park, and he also made his first trip as a paying customer to see 'the Championships' at Wimbledon. Sam Perry agreed to buy his son an old racket for five shillings, and with his natural aptitude for ball games Fred was soon showing promise on court.

The teenage Perry tested himself in serious competition for the first time in 1927. Despite arriving with a tatty old racket and playing with his curious hatchet grip, he caused a stir at the Middlesex Junior Championships by reaching the singles final and winning the doubles. Any thoughts that sweeping to the top in tennis would be easy were dispelled when he used his success in the county championships to enter the British junior championships, hosted annually on hard courts at Wimbledon. He was brushed aside early on in the tournament and, worse still, his only racket broke, leaving him upset and embarrassed.

He described himself as a 'competent quarter-finalist' at most junior tournaments; he never became the junior champion of Middlesex, let alone of England. As his father recognised, he had much catching up to do, having come to the game late, and he was also handicapped by his size. He was about five and a half feet in height (with a growth spurt still to come), and he lacked the power of more physically developed, hard-hitting opponents.[8]

Fred's height was less of a problem in table tennis, the sport at which he really excelled as a youngster. His decision to apply for membership of the Herga club in Harrow was influenced by its provision of table tennis facilities as well as tennis courts, and Fred's progress was so rapid that he was soon chosen to represent England against the other home nations. Table tennis as an international sport was still in its infancy in the 1920s – dominated by the likes of Hungary and Sweden – and with relatively few serious participants Perry was soon making inroads at the highest levels of the game.

He found favour with the British aristocrat Ivor Montagu, a prominent player and administrator, and made his first trip abroad with the England team to compete at the world championships in Sweden in 1928. The following year Fred startled observers by defeating the local favourite to take the world title in Budapest, prompting Montagu to reflect on qualities that were to be prominent characteristics of Perry's tennis: speed of thought and action, willingness to adapt and change tactics when necessary, plus boundless determination and self-confidence. Although barely reported upon in Britain, where table tennis had a limited following, Perry had secured a stunning success: at the age of just 19, he was a world champion.[9]

As Fred's passion for sport grew, so too did his reservations about the world in which his father operated. In May 1929, although not yet old enough to vote, he dutifully assisted Sam on the campaign trail in Kettering. Sam had lost the seat in 1924 and was determined to regain it. In the end the hard work paid off and he managed to defeat his Tory opponent, though his return to the House of Commons was overshadowed by a gathering economic crisis that eventually proved too much for Ramsay MacDonald's second Labour government. Sam refused to join MacDonald's call for a cross-party National administration to face the crisis, saying if he did so he would find his portrait hanging in the Conservative Club in Kettering.

Like many Labour loyalists he was swept aside when the National government won a huge majority in 1931, losing his Kettering seat by nearly 9,000 votes. Although Fred was given the task of going round the local factories kissing all the girls – 'not a bad assignment' – he had never warmed to party politics. His experiences of electoral campaigning ultimately left him determined thereafter to 'steer clear of anything remotely political', he wrote in his memoirs. 'And I have never voted since.'[10]

While he never carried forward his father's interest in politics or religion, Fred's family background and upbringing nevertheless had a lasting impact as he matured into adulthood. Throughout his life, Fred was to be characterised, in addition to a love of sport, by numerous traits and attitudes associated with Sam: a strong work ethic; a tremendous desire to succeed; enormous self-belief; and a clear sense of regional and class identity. Fred had lived long enough in Stockport and Wallasey to always refer to himself in later years as being 'north country', part of the explanation he felt for his reputation for plain speaking. He came from a part of the world, he said, 'where we don't call a spade a spade, we call it a bloody shovel!'[11]

He may have had little time for party politics, but Fred also shared his father's instinctive sympathy for the underdog. He disliked elitism and hated anything that smacked of being put upon by those who regarded themselves as his social superiors. He made up his mind early in life that he wasn't going to 'let people tell me what to do'.

His feisty, outspoken personality was to be much to the fore after he took a major decision in 1929. Although he continued to take part in county and national championships for a few more years, table tennis diminished in appeal for Fred once he had conquered the heights of the game. His father echoed this view, and weighed in with a decisive intervention, telling his son of his concern about the amount of time Fred spent in the smoke-filled rooms that often hosted table tennis events. You look, he said, 'like death warmed up…. Why not concentrate on tennis?'[12]

From the summer of 1929 onwards Fred accepted that the time had come to give his full attention to a single sport rather than attempting to combine his twin passions. One thing was certain: his background, ambition and persona meant he would soon be ruffling feathers in the genteel world of British tennis.

2

Entering the world of elite tennis

I N A BBC Radio 5 Live retrospective of 1999 called *Sporting Century*, Fred Perry was described as an 'unlikely Wimbledon hero'. He certainly faced an uphill battle to be accepted on the British tennis scene. The game originated in its modern form in the Victorian period as a leisure pursuit for the English upper-middle classes, and although it spread rapidly after 1900 to many parts of the globe, it usually remained the preserve of the wealthy. Many of those who became Wimbledon legends in the 1920s and beyond were from backgrounds that contrasted sharply with Perry's humble origins.

The American Bill Tilden, who took the Championships by storm in 1920, was in the words of his biographer 'a Philadelphia patrician'; he was 'urbane, well read, a master bridge player, a connoisseur of fine music'.[1] Perry's opponent in the 1934 Wimbledon final, 'Gentleman' Jack Crawford, was born on a large, prosperous farm in Australia with its own tennis court. In two subsequent finals Perry defeated the German aristocrat Baron Gottfried von Cramm (full name: Gottfried Alexander Maximilian Walter Kurt von Cramm), who was renowned for his exemplary court manners, never questioning or looking upset by any line call or bad decision. It was once reported that at a critical moment in an important doubles match, the ball flew past von Cramm and landed out. The score was called, but the baron signalled to the umpire that the ball had brushed his hair; the point, and subsequently the match, was lost on an issue of honour.[2]

In Britain, tennis remained resolutely well-to-do after the Great War. The home of the game, the All England Club at Wimbledon, was renowned for its small and socially exclusive membership. Based on a four-acre site in Worple Road, the AEC hosted an annual tournament from the 1870s onwards that grew steadily in popularity while maintaining a distinctive garden-party atmosphere. Initially the majority of participants were home-based, but after 1918 the number and success rate of overseas competitors rose sharply.

Wimbledon became a truly international event, and British triumphs against the world's elite became the exception not the rule. With expansion on the original site out of the question, the AEC in 1922 completed a move to a more spacious home in Church Road. Much, however, remained the same. The relinquishment in the 1920s of the title 'the world championships on grass courts', adopted in 1913, did not matter as Wimbledon retained a unique appeal for players, crowds and administrators.[3]

From elite down to club level, tennis in Britain also remained firmly attached between the wars to an amateur ethos. Amateurism – the notion of sport being played for pleasure not profit – had emerged from the public schools and universities during the second half of the 19th century, the period when many major sports pioneered in Britain were being exported throughout the world. Some writers have questioned the link between amateurism and 'fair play', pointing out that the most famous sportsman of the Victorian period, the cricketer W.G. Grace, was notorious for his desire to win at all costs.

But in tennis the prominence of the likes of Crawford and von Cramm illustrates that attachment to amateur ideals remained strong. An instruction book on the game published in 1924 asserted that good sportsmanship and court manners were closely linked, 'every umpire's and linesman's decision, whether right or wrong, must be taken without a murmur.... Playing to the gallery ... is an unforgivable sin.'[4]

At the administrative level, the overwhelming majority of national associations on the International

Lawn Tennis Federation (ILTF) – formed in 1913 to govern the game worldwide – believed that 'professionalism' smacked of the corrosive influences of money and excessive competitive spirit. The upstanding gentlemen who dominated the LTA in Britain, often those with high-ranking military backgrounds, insisted on a strict set of rules.

Among other things, amateurs in lawn tennis were prohibited from playing for any prize money or wagers; from playing in any matches or demonstrations against professionals; selling any prizes won; or receiving any expenses beyond the bare minimum laid down in the rulebook. As in many sports, the regulations served to highlight and reinforce ingrained social divisions. Amateurs were regarded as being above the need to earn money from the game, while professionals were in effect confined to a small number of coaches and groundsmen. In the words of Basil Reay, a leading tennis administrator for much of the 20th century, the nub of the issue was that 'an amateur was a gentleman, a professional was an artisan'.[5]

The archetypal gentleman amateur remained alive and well in the upper echelons of British tennis after the First World War. No one illustrated the continuing spirit of amateur idealism more than Max Woosnam, the son of a clergyman who secured Blues in six different sports when at Cambridge before the war and who survived to win top honours in a range of sports after 1918. As well as capturing two medals in tennis at the 1920 Olympics, winning the men's doubles at Wimbledon and captaining Britain's Davis Cup team, Woosnam was an excellent footballer, playing for England and Manchester City, and he was no slouch at cricket, once scoring a century at Lord's.

Woosnam was famed both for his skill and his adherence to a code of fair play. In his eyes, sport was an enjoyable distraction from his business interests, and he counted himself lucky that his employers were generous in granting him time away from work to compete. In his centenary history of the Northern Tennis Club in Manchester – with which Woosnam had links – David Allaby comments on Max's 'cheerful, unassuming nature', and his habit of taking in a hearty lunch and tankard of beer before taking to the field of play: 'His sense of fun was as undiluted as his favourite pre-match beverage.'

Allaby could not resist contrasting this relaxed attitude with the approach Perry was to bring to the sport, 'Tennis to Fred Perry was never about pit-pat exchanges after a cream tea or chit-chat over cocktails. He trod on one or two toes on his march through the ranks.'[6]

How was it that Perry could even begin to contemplate a 'march through the ranks' in elite amateur tennis? His upbringing meant the odds were heavily stacked against him, and his no-nonsense combativeness put him entirely out of step with the social etiquette of the game. He could not count on inherited wealth to allow him to play at leisure, as could rivals such as Tilden or von Cramm, and as tournament play did not permit prize money, he was always mindful of the need to earn a living.

The last Englishman to win Wimbledon, Arthur Gore, was a quintessential gentleman-amateur, a hard-working businessman who could afford to take time off work at regular intervals without suffering undue financial consequences. Like most of his rivals, Gore travelled under his own steam to Wimbledon, fitting matches around his work schedule and expecting nothing more than the usual rewards on offer for winning the tournament: a trophy, a medal and a shopping voucher.

Although he encouraged his son to develop his sporting talent, Sam Perry still expected that Fred would spend most of his time building a salaried career. After he left school in the mid-1920s, Perry junior secured a post – 'thanks to my father' – as a clerk in the tea department of the English and Scottish Joint Co-operative Society in London. The idea was that he might train for a year before going to India or Ceylon to gain experience on the tea plantations. But Fred quickly realised this was not for him, and he switched to working in Cheapside for Spaldings, a major sporting goods company. Employment in a sports shop brought him closer to where his interests lay, but a routine position with long hours and low pay, a meagre £4 a week, was not one that was likely to facilitate a rise to top-flight tennis.

One of Perry's contemporaries, Ted Tinling – who as the son of a chartered accountant had a more conventional tennis background for the period – later wrote that it was Fred's iron determination that explains his success in fighting his way past the barriers of social discrimination. 'The fact that he finally succeeded in forcing people to accept him,' Tinling claims, 'was due entirely to his belief in himself.'[7]

While Perry's immense inner drive was vital, it should not be overlooked that other forces were at work in explaining his rise to prominence. These included good luck at critical moments (some already noted), but also post-1918 changes in lawn tennis and in society more broadly. With profits from ticket sales at major international tournaments rising, it grated with leading performers such as Bill Tilden and the French 'empress of the court' Suzanne Lenglen that they were officially entitled to nothing more than prize vouchers for their role in popularising the sport.

After losing patience with their respective national associations, first Lenglen and then Tilden accepted offers from American businessmen to embark on well-remunerated exhibition tours. Although immediately banned from the amateur game, a precedent had been set that was to have ramifications in due course for Perry. Unlike before the Great War, it was now possible for a select few to earn money openly and above board through tennis other than via the poorly remunerated routes of coaching or court maintenance. Most top players remained anxious to prove themselves at prestigious amateur events such as Wimbledon. But from the late 1920s onwards there was a version of tennis that could at least theoretically challenge the established game.

As for societal change facilitating the emergence of Perry, it also mattered that slowly, almost imperceptibly, the playing base of tennis was becoming broader after 1918. The tennis historian Digby Baltzell notes that in the USA the best players were increasingly drawn from the 'democratic' Californian system (and from ordinary backgrounds) rather than the 'staid and snobbish…clubs along the Eastern Seaboard'.[8]

Even in Britain the social basis of the game was not altogether unchanging. An enormous growth in the popularity of tennis saw the number of clubs affiliated to the LTA almost double from the mid-1920s to reach an inter-war peak of over 3,200 by 1938. One factor behind this was a steady expansion of the numbers classified by employment type as belonging to the middle classes. The traditional middle class of businessmen, lawyers, doctors, clergymen – often founder members of new tennis clubs in the late-Victorian and Edwardian periods – were increasingly being joined by those regarded as lower-middle class: clerical and shop workers, civil servants, teachers and engineers.

In spite of Sam's working-class origins, the family's well-appointed rented home in Ealing after 1918 had much in common with the millions of privately owned houses being built to accommodate the rise of the middle classes between the wars. In later life Fred referred to what he called his 'lower-middle class' background. As Robert Winder writes in his study of the new sporting generation in post-war Britain, which included golfer Henry Cotton as well as Fred, these rising stars were part of the 'thrusting make-something-of-yourself class… energetic, clean-cut and ambitious'.[9]

The likes of Fred were not out of place, as a result, at some of the tennis clubs springing up after the war as an integral feature of suburbia. As well as belonging to the Herga club in Harrow, in 1928 Perry joined the Chiswick Park club, which in addition to being close to his Ealing base, was – unusually for the time – a congenial home for aspiring young players. Here he could feel confident that his age and background was less important than his playing standard.

While still dominated by the wealthier, more established sections of the middle class, British tennis was not entirely off limits to the likes of Fred. His experience contrasts tellingly with that of Dan Maskell, later to become famous as the voice of the BBC's tennis commentary. Maskell was born the year before Perry, in 1908, and as children, the two had much in common.

Maskell described himself in his memoirs as a 'simple working-class boy', one of a family of eight children from a poor family in Fulham. The Maskells were hard-working but not in the process of moving up the social scale as rapidly as the Perrys after 1918. Leaving school at an early age, Dan was grateful that the prestigious Queen's Club, located in Baron's Court not far from the Maskell family home, provided him with employment. He started as a ball boy and gradually progressed during the 1920s to reach the status of head coach. Even as a prominent coach, however, Maskell remained excluded from certain areas of Queen's Club such as the members' bar. 'In those upstairs, downstairs days of strict social protocol,' he recollected, 'the professionals were not allowed to mix socially with members on the club premises… It was simply the way things were.'[10]

The contrast between Maskell and Perry suggests that, aside from involvement in coaching, tennis as a serious competitive sport continued to be alien territory for the majority of the working classes. The costs of membership (not to mention the rules and prevailing culture) made joining a club forbidding for those who on the basis of being engaged in manual rather than mental labour made up the bulk of the population. Tournament entrance fees, averaging a couple of pounds, plus travel costs to reach venues, were luxuries those on low incomes would hesitate to contemplate. Most of the young aspirants with whom Perry locked horns in his early days in tennis were therefore, almost inevitably, from markedly different backgrounds to his own.

One such was Edward (Ted) Avory, born just a month after Fred in 1909. The Avory family home in Cobham, Surrey, had three courts on which to practise; as Ted later said, he was born 'with a silver tennis racket in his hand'. He also had the luxury, unlike Perry, of opportunities to play that came with his education. Avory was private-school educated before going to Cambridge, where he secured his Blue and was holder of the university title. After leaving Cambridge, Avory was in a position to compete in top events at home and abroad secure in the knowledge that a job was lined up for him at his grandfather's firm on the stock exchange; obtaining time off to play tournaments such as Wimbledon would not be an issue.[11]

Stock market connections were also prominent in the life of Henry Wilfred Austin, the most successful of the emerging British players at the end of the 1920s. Austin's father worked in the City, and with a tennis club near to the family residence in the leafy suburbs of south London, young Wilfred, born in 1906, progressed rapidly to become winner of junior Wimbledon at the age of 16. After prep school he went to a well-regarded independent school, Repton in Derbyshire, where he acquired a nickname, 'Bunny', that stuck for life. In the spring of 1926, while still in his first year as an undergraduate in Cambridge, Austin reached the final of the British Hard Court Championships at Bournemouth; the premier event in the domestic tennis calendar outside of

Wimbledon. In 1928 he reached the last 16 at Wimbledon at his first attempt, prompting speculation that he might be the man to end the long wait for a British winner at the Championships. By 1931 he had risen to second in the unofficial world rankings, and a year later he reached and lost in the first of two appearances in the Wimbledon final.

Bunny Austin, at three years his senior, was to feature prominently in Perry's career. 'I first met Fred in 1929 at the Dulwich Covered Courts,' he later recalled, 'where I often used to practise. "Hello," said Fred as we shook hands, "I'm the table tennis champion of London, Middlesex and the world!"'

Aside from his brashness, Austin was struck at the time by how strong the table tennis influence remained on Perry's style. In effect he felt Perry had simply transferred to the court the shots he played on the table, 'the flicked forehand, the stabbed backhand'. In the view of Austin, although 'wild', Perry already had the attributes of strength and confidence that marked him out as a future champion.

For his part, Perry was to say he did not have a 'scrap of envy' about Austin's more privileged background, though he also admitted it was as much as he could do to understand the 'southern plummy accents' of Austin and his ilk. Despite their growing friendship as they became mainstays of Britain's Davis Cup team, the social gap always remained. Austin later wrote, 'I never had any doubt of Fred's affection for me, but I also knew I was something of a mystery to him. "Bunny and his bloody Shakespeare," he used to say. I enjoyed poetry and often visited the art galleries of the European capitals we played in and generally behaved in what was to Fred an odd manner.'[12]

While the middle-class credentials of most top British players continued to be impeccable, there were a few exceptions. Aside from Perry, the major case in point was G.P. (Pat) Hughes, a doubles specialist and winner of various domestic and international titles such as the Italian Championships. From humble beginnings, Hughes obtained a Bachelor of Commerce from London University and worked for a sports manufacturer, giving him the chance to travel and play overseas. In the view of Teddy Tinling, Pat Hughes – like Perry – 'felt himself a marked man because of the way he spoke', and faced criticisms from some within the game that he was being paid to play via his employment, in breach of the spirit of amateurism. Again like Fred, with whom he was to forge a successful doubles partnership, Hughes faced an uphill battle to gain acceptance in the corridors of power. In a magazine article written in the late 1940s, he reflected with some bitterness on what he saw as the hypocrisy and double standards of the pre-war authorities. 'The game was to be kept "clean" was the official attitude,' even though no similar attacks were made according to Hughes on another (unnamed) player who was a

Cambridge Blue – and 'therefore above suspicion' – who worked for a rival sports company.[13]

The chances of someone from Perry's background making it to the top in tennis were thus slim, but not impossible. If Hughes had employment that was more conducive than Perry's to facilitating tournament play, one advantage the latter had was that he found an encouraging mentor. Unlike in modern-day tennis, coaches or trainers dedicating themselves full-time to individual players were almost unknown in the 1920s.

At his local club Perry was fortunate to come under the wing of A.R. Summers, who worked for the Slazenger sports company and whose fatherly influence earned him the nickname 'Pops'. Summers had a reputation for spotting young, talented players, and from early on in the relationship Perry respected the older man and listened to his advice. In the long run the benefits for Fred were considerable. He obtained valuable advice on technique and how to win matches, he was relieved of the need to worry about buying rackets and equipment – henceforth supplied by Slazenger – and he also had an adviser who could help him plan his itinerary and guide him through the minefield of tennis etiquette. As Ted Tinling noted, the key role of Summers was that he was there to 'take the black sheep into the fold'.[14]

With the guidance of his new advisor, Perry spent the spring of 1929 entering senior tournaments, making sufficient progress to come through three qualifying rounds and thereby reach the main draw at Wimbledon. Although enthralled by the venue and the tournament, his early experiences in SW19 were not always happy ones. In his initial appearances, as elsewhere in the tennis world, he was sometimes made to feel unwelcome, notably when he was the subject of malicious pranks such as removing his clothing from the dressing rooms to disrupt his preparation; the culprit or culprits were never discovered.

At least in 1929, unlike when he played on the hard courts at Wimbledon in the national junior championships, it did not end in tears. Making his senior debut on Court 16 he beat an Italian player, Roberto Bocciardo, in five sets in the first round and then eased past his fellow countryman Norman Dicks in four sets. In the third round he went down in four sets to John Olliff, another British rival 'from the other side of the fence – public school'.[15]

Although Perry's performance barely registered with journalists at the time, Fred Burrow, the tournament referee, later observed that it was quite unusual for a qualifier to win through two rounds. Perry, it would seem, had taken an important step forward in his quest to emulate what he had already achieved in table tennis. In the words of Burrow, the youngster 'had no reason to be dissatisfied with his first appearance at Wimbledon'.[16]

3

On the rise

B Y PROGRESSING through the early rounds at Wimbledon in 1929, Fred Perry showed he was a 20-year-old with potential. But what were his chances of making a real mark in the sport? Tennis was littered with promising young players who fell by the wayside, and there was still some way to go before he could be regarded as a serious force in British, let alone world, ranks.

As well as an astute mentor, another factor in his favour was that he was developing a style of play that was capable of troubling many opponents. As a novice junior, knowing little different, Perry had adopted an approach of safe retrieval, looking to keep the ball in court for long spells. But this brought limited dividends: it left him vulnerable to muscular adversaries who hit past him or forced him into errors. It was Pops Summers who first suggested that he should as a matter of course take the ball earlier after its bounce as a way of speeding up his game. As Fred's forehand was clearly his stronger side it made sense to make the early-ball on that wing the cornerstone of his game.

At the time the only world-class player who regularly employed the early ball technique was Henri Cochet, Wimbledon champion in 1927 and 1929. Perry set about finding out all he could about the Frenchman, and it may have been no coincidence that he was attracted to a player who was largely self-taught and did not possess the background of the traditional gentleman amateur.

Perry's strong wrist and continental grip eventually enabled him to emulate Cochet with what became one of the most potent shots in 1930s tennis. But it was no easy task. There was much hard practice and many frustrations over the winter of 1929 and 1930 before Perry made progress with the early-ball forehand. Nor should it be forgotten that he had other important attributes in his game. His willingness to stay back and trade ground shots or come into the net to volley according to the circumstances gave him greater variety than many players of the era.

In general terms British and American players, reared on fast grass or concrete courts, favoured serve-and-volley tactics and were reluctant to spend too much time at the back of the court. By contrast, most Europeans and South Americans, used to clay surfaces, relied heavily on ground strokes and made only occasional forays to the net. Like the legendary Bill Tilden, Perry had a genuinely all-court game, combining sharp attack with sound defence, as circumstances required. He was, as the *New York Times* called him, a player for 'all surfaces, seasons and continents'.[1]

In addition, Fred allied an ideal physique – lean and increasingly tall – with tremendous fitness, this at a time when it was not always fashionable to be so in amateur sport. According to Pat Hughes, some of his opponents were left floundering by his superior footwork and positioning. One of the reasons his forehand became so feared was that he was rarely off balance when he played it. By great footwork and 'perfect judgment of distance', Hughes wrote, he was nearly always able to step into the ball with a full swing of the racket.

Underpinning Perry's speed and his increasing strength and stamina, as he continued to mature, was a lifestyle that included early nights – at least when tournaments were in progress – and abstinence from alcohol apart from on a few rare occasions (a habit that earned him the nickname 'Monsieur Limonade' in France). On his 21st birthday he collected £100 from his teetotal father, who had promised him the money if he reached that age without drinking alcohol. He also largely refrained from smoking, a hugely popular custom at the time; he carried around a pipe though tended to 'fiddle with it more often than I smoked it'.[2]

The seriousness with which Perry took his chosen sport, with careful attention to diet and drink, pointed to another of his distinctive attributes: his immensely powerful will to win. Part of his drive to succeed included attention to the psychology of the game. In time he was to become a master of whatever advantage was possible through mind games. This was prominent in the advice he later passed on to aspiring players. It was vital, he said, to 'call the tune' by imposing one's own game; if a rival preferred to 'play fast', for example, then 'slow them down'.

This entailed spending a lot of time (again not common in the inter-war period) studying the style of opponents, trying to ascertain what they did or didn't like. As his career progressed, Perry acted on this by manoeuvring opponents into giving him as many short balls on his forehand as possible, knowing that this gave him the opportunity to use his trademark shot to either hit a winner or put in an approach shot that allowed him to take up a strong position at the net.

The psychological side of the game also involved using various techniques of gamesmanship, some more subtle than others. Perry, appearing to mimic Bill Tilden, would often say in a loud voice to opponents after a few minutes of warming up, 'any time you're ready', indicating that he himself was always prepared for the battle to commence. Even the smallest advantage, Perry calculated, was worth having.[3]

Perry's strong desire to win was not of course unusual in top-level tennis. But his refusal to conceal his ambition, in the traditional manner of the gentleman amateur, helps to explain – when combined with his background – why in Britain he struggled to win admirers. His behaviour and demeanour on court in the early days often attracted adverse comment. Norah Cleather, who worked behind the scenes at the AEC, said that when Perry first appeared at Wimbledon he was 'highly-strung, temperamental, mercurial', and displayed several 'bad habits', for example glaring at the umpire and at photographers on the side of the court.[4]

Ted Tinling, who was well attuned to the unwritten codes of behaviour, told a story that highlighted how Perry's implacable need to win at all times made him an outcast in certain quarters. It was common for visiting teams to play friendly matches in the summer against Cambridge University, where the serene atmosphere was usually only punctured by ripples of polite applause and muted calls of 'jolly good shot'. But after Perry went a couple of times with his Chiswick Park team 'it was politely suggested', Tinling recounts, 'that it might be best not to include him in future matches'.

Dan Maskell, who began to practise widely with Perry and other promising juniors after taking up the role of full-time coach at the AEC, felt that in many respects he was not 'typically British', as there was an aggressiveness and dedication about him that was out of line with the conventional attitude towards the sport.[5]

At the beginning of 1930, Perry was still far from being the finished article. While aspects of his game such as his powerful forehand were developing fast, others needed further attention, notably his backhand, and his volatile temperament still made him vulnerable in tight situations. He was essentially a raw, talented youngster with enormous promise; an awkward customer who most of his contemporaries on the tennis scene hoped to avoid, on and off court.

In spite of his great desire to succeed, there were considerable obstacles to him advancing further, and early in 1930 he was badly affected by a huge personal setback: the sudden death of his mother following a short illness. For a while tennis inevitably took a back seat as the family came to terms with the loss, though with his father's backing it was decided that Fred should enter the British Hard Court Championships, held at Bournemouth each year around Easter.

In order to compete at Bournemouth, Perry needed to obtain time off work. But he now encountered another significant problem. The head of the tennis department at his employers, Spaldings, had already arranged to go to Bournemouth to socialise and watch some tennis; Perry was refused leave of absence. His chances of making a name for himself would be severely compromised if he could not participate in one of the main events of the short British season. It was at this point that Perry benefited from the second of three crucial pieces of good fortune (in addition to the lucky breaks he identified). Spurred into action by the likelihood of his son missing the championships, Sam Perry agreed to subsidise Fred's tennis for a year. It was not an easy decision. Financially, it meant a commitment of at least £10 a week – more than twice the weekly wage Perry received in his job, which he immediately resigned from – to cover the cost of tournament fees, travel and living expenses as he played on the circuit with a view to making inroads and qualifying again for Wimbledon. If Fred could concentrate on tennis alone for the 12 months ahead, Sam calculated, it would become clear whether or not he had it in him to reach the very top echelons of the game.

When the decision became known, although parliamentary colleagues of all parties were supportive, it did occasion criticism from some newspapers that a Labour MP was paying for his son to participate in tennis when others had to combine play with work to finance themselves. Sam was unrepentant, and the importance of his resolve cannot be underestimated. This crucial moment deserves more attention than it has hitherto received. Fred was given a one-off opportunity to compete on equal terms against top-quality opposition, and at the same time his desire to make a real impact in the game was reinforced. When he published an account of his career to date in 1934, Perry dedicated the book to 'My Father, who gave me my chance in lawn tennis'.[6]

An early reward for Sam's faith came when Fred exceeded expectations at the championships. He not only made it to Bournemouth; he came within a whisker of taking the title. In the final he lost a long match to Bunny Austin, going down after holding a match point in the fifth set.

Although Perry and Austin were to gradually develop mutual affection and respect, in 1930 they were serious rivals. Austin was everything that Perry was not. In addition to his affluent upbringing, Austin played the game in a classical style from the back of the court, with carefully crafted shots on both forehand and backhand. Perry later wrote that whereas his own game was not pleasing to purists, Austin's stroke play came 'straight out of the instruction manual, line for line, word for word'. Perry was inconsolable after the defeat in Bournemouth. It felt, he said, like a 'black tragedy'. But Pops Summers, driving his young charge back to London, broke the silence in the car by telling Fred that defeat was no bad thing; victory would have prematurely raised expectations too high, and 'I think you'll be ready by the end of the year.'[7]

Although not a message he wanted to hear at the time, it was quickly borne out. In fact a major breakthrough came just a matter of weeks later, shortly after Perry's 21st birthday.

The event that brought his name to much wider attention was Wimbledon in 1930, the year of Bill Tilden's third triumph at the age of 37. Perry secured straight-sets wins in the first two rounds against British opponents, one of them being Brame Hillyard, who was subsequently involved in the AEC dressing room incident after the 1934 final.

He then came up against the flamboyant sixth seed, the Italian baron and First World War flying ace Umberto de Morpurgo. The baron was known as a fierce competitor with a strong forehand and he stormed to a 5-1 lead before Perry pegged him back, taking the first set 10-8. Although Morpurgo took the second set, Perry had a fresh lease of life and rushed through the third 6-1. By this time the crowds, alerted to the prospect of a shock result, were cramming round court three to watch, and they cheered as the young Englishman, using deep cross-court drives and following up to the net, closed out the match 6-2 in the fourth set.

Fred attributed victory to his use of the early-ball technique he had worked on so assiduously the previous winter. The impact of this first high profile win on Perry's career was instantaneous. By chance an LTA selection committee was meeting at Wimbledon the same day, looking to fill the final slot for a small team due to take part in an overseas tour to represent Britain in the autumn. The committee adjourned to watch the end of Perry's match, and awarded him the place on the team when it reconvened.

Victory over Morpurgo also resulted in Perry's first appearance on Wimbledon's famous Centre Court. By surviving to contest the fourth round – one further than on his debut the previous year – he was scheduled on the middle Saturday to meet Dr Colin Gregory, a stalwart of the British Davis Cup team in the 1920s and later an influential chairman of the AEC.

On the morning of the match Perry was summoned to Fred Burrow's office. He suspected that for some reason he was in trouble with the fearsome referee, and would possibly be warned about his conduct. But instead Burrow offered to accompany him on to the deserted show court ahead of the crowds coming in, so that he could stroll around and get used to the atmosphere. Despite this kind gesture, it was a nerve-wracking experience, though Perry put up a good showing before losing to his more experienced opponent in five sets. He conceded afterwards that he struggled to find any consistency during the match, being distracted by the appearance in the royal box of King George V, making one of his rare visits to Wimbledon. There was some consolation, however: Bunny Austin was knocked out at the same stage of the tournament.

Selection for the autumn tour, beginning in the United States, relieved Sam Perry for the time being of any additional financial commitment to his son, as the LTA traditionally covered travel and accommodation costs and expenses for such tours. Boarding the ship *Mauretania* at Southampton, Fred, alongside other young British hopefuls such as John Olliff and Harold

Lee, was immensely proud to be wearing the white team blazer with the Union Jack crest. There were clearly those within the tennis hierarchy who harboured doubts about the last-minute addition to the team.

Not long after leaving port, Perry was summoned by the husband of Kitty Godfree, who won the ladies' singles at Wimbledon in 1924 and 1926. Leslie Godfree was in the tradition of plain-speaking tennis administrators who came from military backgrounds. 'The Major', as he was often called, wanted to establish at the outset who was in charge. No doubt aware of Perry's reputation for waywardness, he told the newcomer that the expectation was not for him to necessarily win many matches on tour but to work hard and learn.

It was a measure of Perry's desire to succeed that he accepted Godfree's lecture almost without question. The benefits of knuckling down became apparent on court after the team's arrival in New York. In this, his first exposure to dealing with conditions in different parts of the world, Perry had to adapt to the intense American heat in September – 'we all felt like wet rags' – as well as to the more unreliable bounce on many of the grass courts when compared with Wimbledon.

At Forest Hills in Queen's, the home of the American national championships, he found a further distraction was that the main arena contained two courts. Although during finals only one court was used, there were occasions when concentration could be upset by applause suddenly breaking out at the end of a point on the adjacent court. Another key feature of the tour was that for the first time it gave Perry sustained experience of playing against the leading Americans. In an England v United States match held before the national championships, he first met and lost to a young Californian, two years his junior, Ellsworth Vines, going down in a long three-set tussle.

'Elly', as he was often known, like Perry was not in the mould of the traditional amateur gentleman. His father abandoned the family when Elly was a small child, leaving his mother to bring up two sons alone. Vines started playing on public courts at the age of 13, and although he had a sullen appearance on court he had a will to win that few could match. Perry formed a close bond with the Californian in time, but in the short term he was a tricky adversary.

'We were destined to meet again and again,' Perry wrote in 1934, 'indeed I think that my friend Ellsworth has stood in the way of my ambitions oftener than any other foreign player.'[8]

In the main US Championships, Perry could be satisfied with surviving, as he had earlier in the summer at Wimbledon, until the fourth round, where he lost in four sets to the experienced American Johnny Van Ryn. Altogether this first leg of a long autumn tour proved extremely rewarding, giving Perry extended high-level competition once the British grass court season had ended.

Aside from the benefits to his tennis, the American trip proved a memorable experience in another way. Perry was bowled over by the wealth and the standard of living he found in the United States, at least among those well-to-do sections of east coast society associated with lawn tennis. Even in the aftermath of the Wall Street Crash, the popularity of the sport was undiminished in America, and it was the custom to provide lavish hospitality to overseas teams of the sort Perry represented.

It was not only the place that had an appeal for Fred; it was also the people. Many Americans, he felt, shared his own outlook, on tennis and on life. From the time of first setting foot in the country, Perry discovered an environment that he felt matched his personality. He was not averse to describing Americans in much the way as he saw himself, 'direct...outgoing, quick on the uptake, [with] lots of repartee', the latter not always being of the 'right sort' in the eyes of more buttoned-up types. It was not surprising that among a later generation of players, Perry was often to be compared with America's Jimmy Connors. They were both, claims Ted Tinling, 'brash, arrogant, cocky, and belligerent'.[9]

From the USA, Perry and Harold Lee embarked on another leg of the autumn tour in South America, joining up with three or four other British youngsters to play in Brazil, Argentina, Chile and Uruguay. Victory in the match against the Brazilians brought the standard cup and a gold fountain pen, the type of prizes he was becoming accustomed to receiving. The standard of play was not as high as in North America, and aided by the retirement of Lee with an injury, Perry won the national championships in Argentina. Although, as he recognised, it was not a first-class honour in the eyes of the tennis world, it was satisfying to claim his first title outside Britain.

After the personal tragedy of the loss of his mother and the questions over whether he would be able to continue playing top-level tennis, the second half of 1930 had seen Perry go from strength to strength, and after five months away he reached home shores just before Christmas confident that the future looked bright. His next ambition, harboured for some time, was to see if he could break into Britain's national team – the Davis Cup squad.

4

Davis Cup drama

THE relentless rise of international competition in tennis provided an important backcloth to Perry's advancing career. Alongside burgeoning press and public interest in national championships, the Davis Cup acted as a key catalyst in stimulating international competition. Before the rise to pre-eminence of football's World Cup after the Second World War, the Davis Cup was regarded as one of the leading events in the global sporting calendar, rivalled only by the Olympics.

Dwight Davis was a Harvard student who in 1900 offered a large silver punchbowl as the prize for a contest based around national teams, without any idea at the time of how 'the Cup' would grow in scale and prestige. Initially only the USA and Britain competed for the trophy, but by 1914 six other nations had entered the fray.

With travel by no means easy or commonplace – journeys between North America and Europe took several days by steamship – Davis Cup matches were usually arranged to coincide with the aftermath of leading tournaments such as Wimbledon, when top players were likely to be gathered together in one place. In line with the increased popularity of tennis after the Great War, the number of participating nations rose sharply, growing to an inter-war peak of 33 in 1928.

The competition was dominated in the early years by the United States, Britain and Australasia, but in 1927 the trophy was won for the first time by France, who for several years thereafter dominated through the prowess of the four 'musketeers': Borotra, Lacoste, Cochet and Brugnon. The importance attached to the Davis Cup helps to explain how in the space of less than a year, during the course of 1931, Perry rose from being a promising young hopeful to a renowned figure in world tennis.

In spite of accusations made by his father's political opponents at election times, Fred was – as Ted Tinling observed – 'a great patriot' as well as an individualist, a lover of royalty from his earliest days.[1] His desire to secure a place in Britain's Davis Cup team was aided when, ahead of the annual trials in the spring of 1931, three members of the squad from the previous year declared themselves unavailable for the season ahead.

As Perry acknowledged, secure in the knowledge of his father's financial backing for the time being, 'it is not everyone who year after year can afford the time' to sacrifice potentially three months to a Davis Cup campaign.[2] Fred was able to earmark his place in the squad by reaching the final of the annual trials, where he again lost to Bunny Austin in a close match. Unusually, he was elated in defeat, knowing he would be representing his country, though he recognised that expectations were low. Britain had not won the cup since before the First World War and seemed incapable of threatening the ascendancy of the Americans and the French.

In spite of a reasonable draw in the European Zone of the competition, due to begin around Easter, the squad – consisting of Austin, Perry, and doubles specialists Pat Hughes and Charles Kingsley – looked weaker on paper than some of its predecessors. It was certainly inexperienced at handling the pressure that came with the unique format of the Davis Cup. As today, ties took place over three days, with two singles on the first and last days interspersed by a doubles on the middle day; a single point for each 'rubber' meant that unless a team took a 3-0 advantage, there would still be all to play for on day three.

The non-playing captain of the team was Herbert Roper Barrett, twice a singles finalist at Wimbledon in his earlier days and in charge of the national team since 1924. He was a strict disciplinarian of the old-school variety, feared and respected rather than loved, and he insisted on high standards of behaviour and decorum. He slowly built a strong bond with Perry, eclipsing Pops Summers in the role of mentor, at least in the Davis Cup arena, though it was not clear at the outset how the fiery young Perry would react to another authority figure laying down the law. Roper Barrett no doubt had reservations of his own. Tinling got the sense that the attitude of those in charge of the squad was 'very much one of "as we've got to have the bloody upstart, we might as well knock him into shape and try and get the best out of him"'.[3]

Almost by accident, in view of the need to build a new team, the British stumbled upon a successful formula for the 1931 campaign. At the age of 21, Fred made his debut in an easy victory on grass against Monaco at Plymouth in April. The opposition, Perry noted, 'were badly affected by the depressing weather', and garnered only 21 games in the 15 sets that resulted in a 5-0 win. This was followed as the summer progressed by four more victories in the European Zone (organised to include non-European teams outside the American Zone) – against Belgium in Brussels, at home against South Africa and Japan and then against Czechoslovakia in Prague. In each of them Perry won both his singles, including successes over accomplished players such as Norman Farquharson of South Africa, who later became the last man to get the better of Fred in singles at Wimbledon.

By reaching the inter-zone final, scheduled for July, the British exceeded expectations. Perry had settled in well, appreciating rather than bridling against Roper Barrett's firm handling, and he forged a strong combination with Austin despite their individual rivalry. Dan Maskell, on hand to coach the team, noted how difficult it was for teams to cope with the two young Englishmen: while Fred hustled and harried his opponents into errors, Bunny drove them to despair 'with his relentless accuracy and imperturbable concentration'.[4]

The British team also developed a habit of prevailing in the crucial doubles rubber. After the Monaco tie, it was decided to try Perry with Pat Hughes in the doubles. As the oldest member of the team, the steadiness of Hughes provided an ideal foil for the youthful aggression of Perry, and their burgeoning partnership carried them to victories in all the remaining European Zone ties. A sense of shared mission was gradually developing. As Perry recollected, Roper Barrett, though hardly 'hail-fellow-well-met', insisted the players should spend the day before any match together rather than on their own, so helping with team bonding across social boundaries.[5]

At first the efforts expended on international duty appeared to have an adverse effect on Perry's individual performances. Making his first appearance at the French national championships in May 1931, he won two matches against lesser-known French opponents after a first-round walkover, but then went out to a wily clay court specialist,

Giorgio de Stefani of Italy. At Wimbledon a few weeks later Perry was in better shape and determined to prove he was edging ahead in the unofficial race between the aspiring British players. He was seeded fifth, one ahead of Austin; the first time there had been two British seeds in the eight-strong men's list since seeding by merit was introduced a few years earlier.

While Austin fell at the quarter-final stage, Perry defeated the American Van Ryn (to whom he had lost twice the previous year) to set up a semi-final clash with the 19-year-old American prodigy Sidney Wood, a player with all the shots, who also cut a distinctive figure playing in plus fours. Although he recovered from a poor start to win the first set, Perry struggled thereafter and Wood closed the match out three sets to one.

For expectant British onlookers, craving home success at Wimbledon after so many years of failure, the result was difficult to bear. 'It was not one of Perry's best days, by any means,' wrote tournament referee Fred Burrow. 'He made far too many mistakes over perfectly easy shots.'[6] Concerns were also expressed, as was the case for some time to come, over Fred's temperament. Whereas Wood remained cool and confident throughout, journalists noted that Perry increasingly lost his composure and argued that he would struggle to claim the top prizes if this trait continued. Perry was not inclined to reach such a harsh verdict on his performance. He had reached a Wimbledon semi-final at only the third attempt – suggesting the potential to go further in future years – and he bowed out at the same stage in both the men's doubles (with Pat Hughes) and the mixed.

In the latter event he and his partner Mary Heeley were leading when Perry tripped over the stone surround of the court. Although he was keen to continue, it was decided that the British pair should concede as a precautionary step with the inter-zone final due to take place just a week later.

It was a measure of how seriously the United States, Britain's opponents in the inter-zone final, themselves took 'the Cup' that Sidney Wood became the only man to win Wimbledon by default when his fellow American Frank Shields was persuaded by team officials not to contest the final because of an injury. Although he benefited from the decision, Wood later derided what he saw as 'the most stupid affront to Wimbledon you could imagine…but our Davis Cup committee were a bunch of old guys with badges'.[7]

The domination of the American men at Wimbledon made them strong favourites for the inter-zone final, though the British had perhaps one thing to their advantage: the venue. As the holders, the French were not required to enter the competition until the grand final, the Challenge Round, held at the location of their choice – Stade Roland Garros in Paris. The musketeers awaited the winners of the inter-zone match, also to be held in Paris, where the clay surface had been installed in part because, unlike the grass of Wimbledon, it helped to nullify the American threat in the Davis Cup. As Arthur Wallis Myers of the *Daily Telegraph* wrote, 'the French court favours finesse', while 'the English court ministers to attacking speed'.[8]

Bunny Austin's measured consistency proved too much in the opening rubber for Sidney Wood, allowing Britain to strike the first blow in the inter-zone final, though this was countered when Frank Shields – speedily recovered from the injury that kept him out of the Wimbledon final – inflicted a rare straight-sets defeat on Perry. In the doubles the Wimbledon winners George Lott and Johnny Van Ryn beat Perry and Hughes to give the Americans a 2-1 advantage going into the final day.

The odds looked stacked against the British, but Perry – courtesy of what he called 'lots of scraping and running' – avenged his semi-final loss to Sidney Wood by beating him in four sets. Wood's natural talent was not always matched by his concentration levels, and from this time on Perry was usually dominant when they met. The momentum of the tie shifted and Austin, Britain's hero on this occasion, swept to a straight-sets victory over Shields in the deciding rubber. It was a huge shock to the established order in world tennis, the first time the Americans had failed to reach the Challenge Round since 1920.

The British were deservedly on a high as, after a couple of days of sightseeing in Paris, the players prepared themselves for taking on the French at the end of July. But it was one thing to overcome the Americans on clay; quite another to get the better of the French. The musketeers had demonstrated great confidence and togetherness in winning the cup four times in succession, and as the tennis journalist Rex Bellamy was later to note, playing at Roland Garros always presented an enormous challenge for outsiders.

What makes it, Bellamy wrote, 'the supreme, all-round test of tennis…is the combination of heat with a loose, gritty surface that, by means of friction, takes the pace off the ball. The quick-footed, violent cut-and-thrust that prospers at Wimbledon…is not good enough for Paris. Rallies last longer. The ball cannot be put away easily. So matches become a prolonged series of tactical manoeuvres containing every trick in the book; every variation of pace and length, spin, angle and trajectory. These sweating, straining endeavours demand both physical and mental stamina. They demand a delicate balance between sparring and a commitment to attack. And the longer a match lasts, the greater the threat of cramp, shrieking agony, even tears.'[9]

The young British team nevertheless gave a good account of itself on the first day of the Challenge Round. Austin lost to the resilient Henri Cochet, but this time it was Perry who excelled with one of the best wins of his career so far, over the legendary Jean Borotra. The Frenchman was renowned for his crowd-pleasing tactics, which included making an extravagant display of putting on a variety of berets from his hat box while changing ends.

In the pressure cooker of the Davis Cup Final, Perry eventually prevailed after a protracted, tense struggle. The match turned when, after losing the first set, Perry held on to take the second 10-8 and then rushed through the third 6-0. Although Borotra rallied in the fourth, his younger opponent had greater staying power, and he was mobbed by his team-mates after capturing the final set 6-4. The price Perry paid was exhaustion, such that Roper Barrett decided he should be rested from the doubles, which was won by the French to give them the advantage on the second day.

Bunny Austin's win over Borotra in the first of the reverse singles meant that, as against the Americans, the British were taking more favoured opponents down to the wire. The irony for Perry was that it meant the decisive rubber was against Cochet, who had been the inspiration for the early-ball technique adopted by the Englishman.

The young pretender still had things to learn, however, about the dark arts of gamesmanship. In his memoirs Perry admitted after his four-set defeat that the man he admired so much 'conned' him with some clever tactics.[10] The French team celebrated the retention of the cup amid the customary shower of cushions thrown on to the court, and although Perry was disappointed, it was far from his most crushing defeat. The British returned home more than satisfied at having reached the Challenge Round for the first time since 1919, and the LTA expressed its pleasure by holding a celebratory dinner at the Savoy hotel.

Fred's emergent status was underlined when in the wake of his cup exertions he was offered the chance to write tennis columns for London newspapers; this was permissible under the amateur rules providing he did not write directly about his own matches, and it enabled Perry to tap into a source of income that was increasingly important to him as his career progressed.

Shortly afterwards, still on the crest of a wave following the Davis Cup experience, Perry set off from Southampton across the Atlantic for an autumn tour in the company of Pat Hughes. It was to be a hugely enjoyable and productive trip for Fred. Within a week of landing, Perry won the Westchester tournament held at Rye, just outside New York, his first singles title in North America. Continuing his vein of good form, Perry beat seven of the top-ten ranked Americans.

He also made a great impression in the American national championships, played on the grass courts in front of the elegant buildings of the West Side tennis club at Forest Hills. He swept past several home players to reach the semi-finals, where he lost to Elly Vines in five sets. Although delighted to reach the latter stages of a major tournament for the second time so early in his career, Perry was faced with barbs about the manner in which he lost the advantage.

Critics alleged that by allowing himself to be upset by a linesman's decision in the middle of the fourth set, he displayed a suspect temperament that let him down at vital moments. This criticism had much credence, though he also had to admit that Vines generally 'had the edge' over him, winning three other encounters that autumn. He was left to hope he might be able to turn the tables should they meet in Europe, 'Where conditions would be more in my favour.'[11]

Despite the carping from some quarters, Perry considered it a 'wonderful tour', and it was not over yet. On his arrival in the US he was already a better-known figure than in 1930 owing to Britain's endeavours in the Davis Cup, and his progress in east coast tournaments made him even more in demand among American officials. Before long he and Hughes were receiving requests to extend their stay, notably from the organisational head of the Southern California Tennis Association (SCTA), Perry Jones, who asked if the British pair would travel to Los Angeles to play in the Pacific Southwest tournament, scheduled to take place every year after the national championships.

Hughes cabled London to secure the permission of the LTA, which agreed to the players travelling west provided they funded themselves; the governing body had budgeted for the costs of the trip to New York and was not in the habit of hastily coming up with additional funding. The SCTA at this point agreed to cover travel and hotel costs, and the players were also discreetly asked about their 'personal terms'.

This was the first occasion on which Perry, accustomed to the strict enforcement of amateur rules by the British LTA, was introduced to the way in which some tournament authorities around the world offered 'under the counter' inducements to attract the best players. Anxious not to fall foul of their own governing body by requesting money, Perry and Hughes gave a flippant response. Both said they would like dates with beautiful young actresses, and convinced that nothing would come of it, Perry expressed a preference for the glamorous star Jean Harlow.

In September 1931 Perry and Hughes thus found themselves taking a luxurious train ride across America, with the vastness of the country leaving a deep impression. This first visit to California was a life-changer for Perry, opening up a whole new world. He was already fond of the east coast, but this latest adventure gave him the chance to become a man-about-Hollywood.

Soon after their arrival Perry and Hughes were installed at the plush Roosevelt hotel, and a car arrived the same evening to take them off to the first of many dinners and parties. Perry recalled he was dumbfounded when the driver went to pick up another guest en route: it was none other than Jean Harlow, looking 'stunning' in a black dress set against her platinum-blonde hair. She proceeded to introduce him to Hollywood, a short drive from the centre of Los Angeles. For a young man aged 22, Perry had to admit he was 'dazzled'.

He was soon mixing with other screen stars, and was invited by the movie boss Jack Warner to visit his studios. The company offered to pick up the tab if they wanted to take any young starlets out to dinner, no doubt calculating that useful publicity photos involving good-looking, smartly turned out tennis players would follow to help generate interest in upcoming films. 'So everybody benefited: Warner, the stars, and F.J. Perry.'[12]

In spite of the distractions of the social scene, Perry's tennis also flourished in California. The concrete courts at the Los Angeles Tennis Club, perched on a hillside with magnificent views of the surrounding area, were ideally suited to his early-ball game. He was confident – much more so than on the grass at Forest Hills – that the bounce would be true. In the first of what was to be five successive visits, he reached the final of the Pacific Southwest tournament, an event where film stars such as Marlene Dietrich and Clark Gable watched on from their private boxes court-side.

Although he lost again to Vines, this time in a close five-set match, it was obvious that Perry was in his element. After the class distinctions and snobbery that he encountered in daily life as well as on the tennis scene in Britain, travelling and working in the United States was hugely liberating and refreshing. He later recollected that he was taken aback by the 'hurry-hurry' pace of life in the States, which 'appealed to me because I'm a fast-acting character'.[13]

Although called home earlier than he hoped to help his father on the general election campaign trail in England, on the whole life could not have been better for the 'hurry-hurry' young Englishman. Tennis was providing plenty of opportunities to travel the world experiencing a variety of lifestyles and cultures; before the winter was out he was to make further trips to represent Britain in Scandinavia and the Caribbean.

What was more, despite being regularly out-powered by Vines in the autumn, Perry had made a meteoric rise in men's tennis. During the course of the year he had reached two semi-finals in major tournaments (and could potentially have been Wimbledon champion by default if he had reached the final, owing to the withdrawal through injury of Frank Shields) and he had played a central role in taking Britain to the Challenge Round of the Davis Cup. He now found himself ranked in the unofficial 'World's First Ten', published in the United States *Official Encyclopaedia of Tennis*, coming straight in to the list for 1931 at number four, behind only Cochet, Austin and Vines. After such an exhilarating year, it looked to be only a matter of time before Perry became one of the sport's elite top three.

5

A year of disappointments

THE WORDS of Rudyard Kipling's poem *If*, about meeting with triumph and disaster and treating these two 'impostors' just the same, are famously well known to Wimbledon hopefuls, inscribed above the players' entrance to Centre Court.

In the next phase of his career, Perry was to experience something of both sentiments. After a year of rapid progress, his advancement stalled in 1932. As his profile rose in the wake of reaching the Davis Cup Final and the latter stages of major tournaments, he was the subject of increasing interest among the press and senior figures in British tennis. Some of the newspaper coverage was highly critical when he did not always perform at the peak of his ability, and bits of advice about his play offered from the sidelines – though well-intentioned – caused him confusion rather than clarity.

Damaging defeats followed, denting at least temporarily Perry's natural ebullience, which some critics felt amounted to over-confidence. If he thought it was simply a matter of time before he stepped up to dominate the world game, then he was mistaken. Whatever the underlying reasons, Perry was unable to make the decisive step forward to become a genuine contender for the top titles. Some caution is therefore required in regarding Perry's rise to pre-eminence as inevitable by this point. There was still much hard graft ahead, and it was not until the middle of 1933 that he moved to the next level.

The 1932 European season began well enough in the spring when he claimed what was to be the first of five successive victories at the British Hard Court Championships at Bournemouth. But a poor run of form began soon after at the French Championships in May. Although he won the mixed doubles title with Betty Nuthall (his first grand slam title), Perry made an unexpected exit in the quarter-finals of the singles. According to *The Times*, he 'seemed wholly to underestimate his man' when he met the eccentric Czech Roderick Menzel.[1]

Perry had beaten his opponent comfortably by playing attacking tennis in the Davis Cup the previous year, but on this occasion he relied on Menzel cracking first in long baseline rallies. As the score fluctuated, with each man claiming two sets, most observers thought Perry looked flat, playing a game that did not suit him. He seemed to be in control at 5-3 in the final set, but after that he never won another game. For the Englishman, it was a severe setback; losing from a winning position in the final set seemed to confirm the view of detractors that Perry's temperament was suspect when the pressure was at its greatest.

Despite the disappointment at Roland Garros, expectations were high when it came to playing on grass at Wimbledon. The hope was that Perry, seeded fourth, would at least match his achievement of the previous year in reaching the semi-finals, and perhaps even go one better this time. In the early rounds he looked in fine fettle, beating British opponents who included Herman David, later to be a distinguished chairman of the All England Club. He was also relatively untroubled in defeating two experienced Americans, Van Ryn and Wilmer Allison.

But as in Paris, Perry came unstuck in the quarter-final, losing in four sets to Jack Crawford. The Australian was at the top of his game in 1932, combining great anticipation with a level of consistency that made him hard to overcome. Once again it was left to the doubles to provide a measure of compensation. In partnership with Pat Hughes, Britain's established Davis Cup pairing reached the final of the men's event, and only lost in five sets to the holders Borotra and Brugnon.

In the summer of 1932, Perry gave every impression of being cast in the mould of many past (and future) British hopefuls: hugely talented, but seemingly lacking the tactical awareness as well as the mental fortitude to turn promise into fulfilment. He was still struggling to step out of the shadow of his rival and Davis Cup team-mate Bunny Austin, who became the focus of national hopes when he made it through to the Wimbledon final. Any prospect of Austin being the man to end the long years of British underachievement at the Championships disappeared, however, when he was crushed by Ellsworth Vines, making his first appearance at Wimbledon.

After overcoming Crawford in the semis, Vines destroyed Austin in a display of stunning power and accuracy, dropping only six games. He served 30 aces, including one at match point so fast that most observers including the umpire spoke of seeing only a puff of chalk on the service line before the ball hit the stand behind his baffled opponent. Duncan Macaulay, an assistant at the AEC, described the final as 'murder on the Centre Court'.[2]

One sobering lesson here for Perry was how far he still needed to improve to match the world's very best. The Wimbledon crown was only one of 11 senior titles claimed by Vines in 1932. Perry was not of course lacking in the commitment required for success and he was making conscious efforts to improve his temperament. During his run of good form in 1931, he tried to replace glaring at umpires or line judges with a more relaxed outward appearance. His frequent joking and caustic one-liners were not always appreciated by opponents, many of whom resented being subjected to this form of gamesmanship.

According to Sam Perry – with Britain having become serious contenders for the Davis Cup – Fred received instructions in 1932 from those who 'should have known better' (diplomatically not named, but associated with the British team) that a more conservative approach would be preferable, 'You must keep up your reputation. Do not smile on the court, it is not done.' This advice, Sam felt, had unfortunate consequences, helping to explain a period in which he felt his son often played too cautiously.[3]

If it was the case that unwelcome interference from the sidelines inhibited Perry's natural game, there was no better example than in July 1932. Earlier in the season Britain had completed comfortable victories in the opening rounds of the Davis Cup, and with Wimbledon out of the way the team headed to Berlin for a European Zone semi-final against Germany. After reaching the Challenge Round in 1931, the British started as favourites. For their part, the Germans hoped to exploit home advantage, choosing to play the tie on slow clay courts at the Ross-Weiss club. They were also stronger than in previous years with the addition to their squad of the emerging talent Gottfried von Cramm, the son of a Hanoverian nobleman.

The Germans certainly got off to a flying start. Bunny Austin was still suffering from the effects of his heavy defeat in the Wimbledon final, and succumbed to the defensive qualities of the German number one, Dr Daniel Prenn. In the first of several encounters with von Cramm, Perry won in straight sets to level the tie, and then, partnered by Pat Hughes, secured the doubles on the second day to give Britain the advantage. But 24 hours later von Cramm got the better of Austin, who in Perry's view on this occasion was 'listless and irresolute'.[4] As in Paris a year earlier, British hopes were resting on Perry in the deciding rubber.

Aside from the pressures that came with the closeness of the tie, Perry was also confronted with some suspect behaviour on the part of German officials. It was one thing that the court was thoroughly soaked beforehand to slow play down to suit Prenn's baseline game; this was the equivalent of British home ties being scheduled on fast grass courts at Wimbledon or elsewhere. The plan worked in that Prenn got off to a good start, taking the first two sets, though as the court dried out Perry came back to capture the third. There followed a ten-minute break in which German guides led the Englishman to and from the changing rooms by a circuitous path, telling him they were trying to avoid the crowds. En route, however, Perry glimpsed his opponent sitting comfortably on a massage table. If the idea was to cause Perry fatigue, this part of the German approach backfired; Fred was so riled by his treatment that he returned full of aggression, taking the fourth set without losing a game and then surging to a 5-2 lead in the fifth.

But the home officials were not finished. At this delicate stage one made what proved to be a decisive intervention. Standing at match point on Prenn's serve, Perry hit a winning return and advanced to the net to shake hands, only to find that a baseline judge had belatedly called a foot-fault. This was the first time in the match there had been a foot-fault problem for either player, and Fred was convinced his German opponent was told to take a second serve as a last-gasp opportunity to keep the match alive.

The replayed point was won by Prenn with a crisp volley and Perry never won another game. Prenn was mobbed as the Germans celebrated, though only a year later the hero of the day was to be removed from the squad as the Nazis sought to eradicate Jews from all public services and the professions. For Perry it was his worst experience yet on a tennis court, 'One point – just one little point – ruined the 1932 season for me.'[5]

Perry may have embroidered some of the account he gave in his later autobiography, but the trauma he went through was fresh in his mind when he reflected on perhaps the bitterest defeat in his career thus far in 1934. He admitted with candour that under huge pressure he had 'cracked'. His despair stemmed in part from letting a match slip when it was so clearly in his grasp. But his dismay was compounded by the knowledge that this was not an individual loss; the defeat of the team inevitably provoked a major inquest.

Hard questions were asked afterwards at home about why Perry lost, and one journalist dubbed Austin and Perry as 'cab horses', a jibe that rankled for a long time. It was several weeks before Perry felt calmer about the defeat and however much he told himself it was only his contribution that kept Britain in the tie until the final rubber, Fred knew his reputation within the British tennis community had been adversely affected.[6]

Some of the criticism he felt smacked of double standards. Perry believed that in some quarters he was singled out for attacks that would not be made on others who conformed more to the model of the gentleman amateur. While it was true that the likes of von Cramm always reined in their emotions, Perry knew that the incomparable Bill Tilden (along with several other top Americans) was not above angry outbursts, and yet was frequently held up for having an ideal temperament. The lesson Perry was learning, painfully, was that he should at least try to disguise his frustrations more expertly.

Setting off for the United States in August 1932 initially brought no relief. Haunted by the loss in Berlin, Perry made little impression in the warm-up tournaments for the American national championships, in contrast to the previous year when he claimed several scalps. At

Newport, Rhode Island, he suffered the indignity of losing to a university student, David N. Jones, ranked only 18th in the United States. What was worse, at Forest Hills he again forfeited a winning position, this time going down to long-standing adversary Sidney Wood in the fourth round. Having taken the first two closely fought sets, Perry didn't win a single game in the third and fourth sets and then lost 7-5 in the decider. It was further proof that he seemed incapable of closing out tight matches.

Despite being a great admirer of all things American, his mood was not improved by some of the company he was obliged to keep off court. Perry travelled as part of a four-man British team to the States, and the varsity background of his colleagues – Austin, Olliff and Avory – meant there were times when he was the odd man out. Avory recalled that the players were wined and dined by east coast society, requiring them to mix with some of America's wealthiest families. Social occasions were sometimes more formal than on the west coast. Not being familiar with the etiquette and local customs, Avory recollected, Perry at a lunch hosted by business tycoon's wife Mrs Vanderbilt 'drank the fingerbowl, to the horror of the hosts and the barely concealed hilarity of his middle-class team-mates'. Irritated at feeling out of place, he was further discomforted when the hostess asked him if he played 'ping pong'. '"If you mean table tennis, madam, I happen to be world champion," was the frosty reply, which silenced Mrs Vanderbilt for the rest of the meal.'[7]

Perry was more deflated than at any time in his career so far, unable to work out in his mind why big matches were slipping through his grasp. Some useful tips eventually came, not from his British colleagues, but from an American friend, Sam Hardy, a former manager of the United States Davis Cup team. After Perry's exit at Forest Hills, Hardy questioned him about why he appeared to have lost some of his edge. When Fred explained he had been advised to adopt 'safety first' tactics and not be too exuberant, Hardy exploded, saying it was 'sheer folly' for others to impose 'anybody else's game and temperament upon you'. The American counselled in the strongest possible terms that Perry would do well to be his old self, and let the results take care of themselves.[8] With a renewed determination to play what he called 'care-free tennis', Fred experienced an upturn in fortunes when he travelled on to California.

On the protracted four-day journey to Los Angeles, there were indications that the more bumptious side of Perry's personality was returning to the fore. The British team was joined on the train by Bunny Austin's wife, the actress Phyllis Konstam, and at breakfast on the first morning she announced that Bunny was suffering a heavy nosebleed and would not be appearing. Ted Avory recalls that Perry muttered something about him being a 'weakling', just loud enough to be overheard.

It was only later discovered that Austin was prone to periodic bouts of jaundice, brought on by a liver defect, which may have helped to explain his superior record in the Davis Cup, where he usually played only two singles and no doubles, compared with the longer grand slam events.

Whether or not it was an extension of his rivalry with Bunny, there was little love lost between Perry and Mrs Austin. Nor was it only middle-class English women who found Perry insufferable at times. Avory was approached at one of the week's glittering events by the famous actress Bette Davis. 'Mr Avory, will you do me a favour? Would you strangle Fred Perry for me?' Avory quipped in return, 'With pleasure, madam, but I will have to stand in the queue.'[9]

On court, Perry emerged victorious in two important tournaments – the Pacific Southwest championships in Los Angeles and the Pacific Coast Championships in San Francisco. Both were successes to savour. It was pointed out by Perry Jones of the SCTA that for the past five years the winner of the event in Los Angeles had gone on to take the American national title the year after, which Perry regarded as a good omen. And at San Francisco there was the satisfaction of beating his rival Austin in four sets in the final.

Yet despite asserting his place as the British number one with this end-of-year victory, and however much his spirits were lifted by returning to Hollywood (the film

colony were 'wonderful people'), there was no disguising
that for Perry 1932 had been, if not exactly a disaster,
then immensely disappointing. He fell in the 'World's
First Ten' from a ranking of four the previous year to
seven. At successive defining stages of the playing season
– at Roland Garros in the spring, in the Davis Cup tie
against Germany in the summer, and at Forest Hills in
the autumn – he had been found wanting at the crucial
stage of long matches.

If for any reason Perry's career had ended at this
point, far from being remembered as a British tennis
legend, he would have been regarded as a nearly man, a
player who promised much but had not fully delivered.
Winning a smattering of tournaments in 1932 was
a creditable addition to his semi-final appearances
at Wimbledon and Forest Hills the previous year, but
detractors believed he would go no further unless he
controlled his emotions more effectively on court. If he
was to shake off a reputation, especially in his homeland,
for not being of the right calibre when the chips were
down, Perry would have to do better in 1933.

6

Triumph in Paris

PERRY WENT into 1933 knowing that something had to change. He had been playing top-level tennis for more than three full seasons, long enough to no longer be regarded as a naïve newcomer. While he could be proud of being counted among the best in the world, he was conscious of being unable to shake off his image as a player who flattered to deceive, who could not quite pull off the victories when the stakes were at their highest.

Brooding on the lessons of his recent five-set losses as he returned home from the United States, Perry embarked on a strategy that was to help propel him – after one or two more false dawns – to a higher level of performance. He decided, crucially, that he would make himself the fittest player on the circuit. His reasoning was that as he was capable of taking at least one set from most opponents, the longer matches lasted the better his chances would become.

To realise his ambition he began a regular training regime with the professionals of the Arsenal football team, the dominant force in English football in the early 1930s. With the assistance of Davis Cup coach Dan Maskell, Perry also made strenuous efforts to improve remaining weaknesses in his game, notably his backhand. Although opponents would always regard this as his weaker wing, Fred worked hard to develop both his up-the-line backhand pass and his short, angled cross-court backhand. In the view of Maskell, long hours on the practice court, allied to training at Arsenal, did much to harden Perry's 'naturally athletic frame, with its God-given slim hips and broad shoulders, into an instrument of sporting destruction'.[1]

But would supreme fitness and improved technique prove the decisive missing pieces of the jigsaw? In the early part of 1933 the indications were mixed. Perry was part of a British team of men and women that lost all three 'test matches' in a short tour of South Africa, prompting concern that another humiliating exit in the Davis Cup might be in store. As automatic choices for the national squad, Perry and Austin were invited to play an exhibition match rather than contesting trials. The following day one national newspaper, developing an earlier line of criticism, described the two players as resembling 'nothing so much as a couple of derelict old cab horses', suggesting the first

21-year-old Perry in action at Wimbledon, June 1930. A raw talent, Fred made a real breakthrough in his fledgling career by beating a top seed en route to reaching the fourth round.

Perry at Victoria Station, setting off to join his Davis Cup team-mates in Paris ahead of matches against the USA and France, July 1933. The British team returned triumphant as Davis Cup champions for the first time since 1912.

Fred holding a clutch of the trophies he won on his winter tour of 1933/34, which included grand slam victories in America and Australia that propelled him to the pinnacle of the men's game.

Perry shakes hands with his Australian opponent, Jack Crawford, after securing his first Wimbledon title, July 1934. Behind the scenes winning Wimbledon was a bittersweet experience for Fred.

King George V and Queen Mary offer their congratulations on a twin British success at Wimbledon in 1934. Fred's win was matched by Dorothy Round, whose victory in the ladies' singles was greeted more rapturously than Perry's by the home crowd.

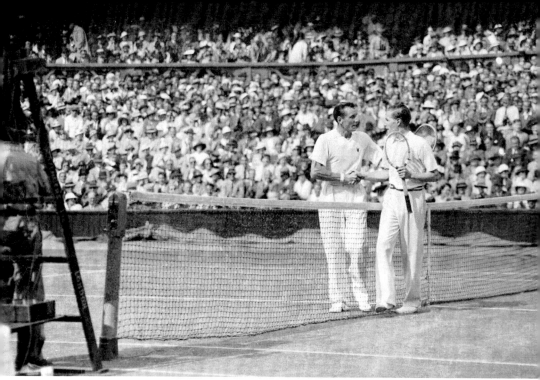

In his second
Wimbledon final in
July 1935, Perry (left)
retained his title with
a straight-sets win over
his elegant German
opponent, Gottfried
von Cramm.

Fred with his first
wife, the Hollywood
actress Helen Vinson,
pictured shortly
after their marriage
in America in the
autumn of 1935.

Perry's natural athleticism is seen here in his last Wimbledon final, where he crushed an injured and out-of-sorts von Cramm, July 1936.

By 1936, as the body language in this photo illustrates, Fred was on relaxed terms with Bunny Austin (left), a fellow stalwart of Britain's Davis Cup team, though earlier in their respective careers they were strong rivals for individual honours.

Perry in action against Adrian Quist of Australia in the Davis Cup Final, played at Wimbledon in late July 1936. This tie, which resulted in Britain's fourth successive Davis Cup triumph, marked Perry's last appearance on the hallowed turf before he left amateur tennis and turned professional.

Pictured from left to right: Ellsworth Vines, Groucho Marx, Charlie Chaplin and Perry at the Beverly Hills Tennis Club, California, July 1937. Perry and Vines teamed up to relaunch the club, home to many of the Hollywood set.

Perry visits Simpson's department store in London, April 1953. By this time Fred had embarked on his most successful and enduring business venture, the Fred Perry sportswear company.

Perry flying into London to undertake a coaching course, pictured with his fourth wife Barbara ('Bobby'), April 1954.

Fred with Barbara at Broadcasting House in London, 1989; BBC Radio Sport hosted a dinner to celebrate his 80th birthday. In the last years of his life Perry's earlier differences with the British tennis establishment were finally forgotten and his achievements fully recognised.

The tennis legend: Andy Murray poses for photographers in front of the Perry statue outside Centre Court, July 2013, after becoming the first British man to claim the Wimbledon title since Fred's trio of 1930s victories.

F J PERRY
WIMBLEDON CHAMPION
1934 1935 AND 1936

DAVID WYNNE
SCULPTOR 1984

round tie against Spain in April might be an opportunity to try out fresh blood. Clearly scars opened by the loss to Germany in 1932 had not yet healed.[2]

The LTA stuck with the same team, which won comfortably in Barcelona, and Perry returned to retain his British Hard Court title at Bournemouth. The spring was busy with further European Zone Davis Cup ties. With home advantage, this time there were no slip-ups and Britain came through comfortably against Finland, Italy and Czechoslovakia. Perry was in good form in most of these matches, continuing his tried-and-tested partnership in the doubles with Pat Hughes, though he did lose one singles against the Italian de Stefani, who repeated the success he had when the two last met at Roland Garros in 1931.

Fred's third appearance at the French Championships in May, however, proved no more successful than the first two. He had a favourable draw and came through the early rounds with ease, but was disappointingly beaten in the quarter-finals by the elegant Japanese player Jiro Satoh. In the words of the *Telegraph*'s Wallis Myers, Satoh was 'a competitor who has Job's patience allied to the wisdom of Solomon', traits which so frustrated Perry that he served two double faults in the final game of a long five-setter.[3]

Perry did secure the men's doubles title with Pat Hughes, but coming away from Paris the question marks remained both over his temperament and his vulnerability when he appeared to be in winning positions.

Concerns were reinforced when at Wimbledon a few weeks later Perry suffered his most serious reverse yet in a major tournament. He had hitherto progressed at least to the third round, but this time he went out in the second round to Norman Farquharson. Usually considered a doubles specialist, the South African prevailed in five sets, mostly by harrying Perry with serve-and-volley tactics. Fred Burrow, the Wimbledon referee, lamented that 1933 was another year in which home players failed to live up to expectations: Perry's loss was a 'a crushing, and most unexpected, blow to English hopes'.[4]

In the wake of this defeat, there was every prospect that Perry's season would fizzle out much as it had done in 1932. Press commentators did not think much of British hopes in the next stage of the Davis Cup, the zone final in mid-July against Australia, who at this time competed (owing to the lack of opponents nearer to hand) in the European section of the cup.

Wimbledon, after all, had been won in superb style by Jack Crawford, defeating the reigning champion Vines. Although Crawford won the first rubber as expected against Austin, Perry levelled things up by hustling a raw 17-year-old – and pioneer of the double-handed backhand – Vivian McGrath, to a straight-sets defeat. The crucial moment came on the second day when Perry teamed up again with Pat Hughes to defeat Turnbull and Quist in four sets. This put Britain in the driving seat for the final day, with Austin able to complete the victory by beating McGrath. It was a job well done: the British were now just one tie away from the Challenge Round.

The inter-zone final against the Americans was scheduled to take place a week later in Paris, and for the first time it was decided that a coach should accompany the British team overseas. In order to preserve social niceties, the LTA booked Dan Maskell into a different hotel from the players, a situation that everyone concerned found embarrassing as they met up daily to practise. Despite this, Maskell found team spirit high, marked by frequent friendly banter, and when the tie got under way the British got off to an excellent start.

Bunny Austin took revenge for his mauling in the 1932 Wimbledon final by using his accuracy and consistency to outlast his more powerful opponent, Ellsworth Vines, whose thunderbolt serve and crunching forehand were blunted on the Paris clay. On the crest of a wave following this unexpected win, Perry followed up with a straight-sets win over the Texan, Wilmer Allison. But the mood of elation in the British camp turned sour the following day when Perry and Hughes were beaten by the American doubles specialists George Lott and Johnny Van Ryn.

Tension was running high on the final day until after two hours Austin took his team over the finishing line by beating Allison in four hard-fought sets, so ensuring Britain reached the Challenge Round for the second time in three years. The postscript was a remarkable personal battle in sweltering heat between Perry and his nemesis,

Vines. The American for some time had been distracted by financial offers to join Tilden's professional tour in the United States. Perry was soon to experience the same type of distractions himself, but in an effort to show he was not quitting the amateur game on the slide, Vines pulled out all the stops against the Englishman. Even though they were playing a 'dead' rubber, both men went full out until the match ended dramatically with Vines retiring after twisting his ankle and collapsing at match point down in the final set.[5]

Any celebrations by the British team were restrained. The players knew they were due to face the French in the Challenge Round the following week so stayed on in Paris to prepare. The mood in the camp, Perry recalled, was buoyant, with good relationships between the team and the non-playing members of the group, who included Tom Whittaker ('of Arsenal fame') and the likeable secretary of the LTA, Anthony Sabelli, in charge of oversight of costs, as well as Roper Barrett and Dan Maskell, the latter finally installed at the same hotel as the others at the players' insistence.

The relaxed mood was illustrated when on a day off playing golf a trick was played on Perry by telling him there was a phone call making him a film offer. His debonair good looks made him increasingly in demand for films and magazines, and he rushed off to take the call, though it turned out to be bogus. In his absence his ball was replaced with a fake one that shattered into pieces when he came back and hit it, much to the amusement of the others.

Although underdogs against the champions on home soil, the British did feel they had one thing in their favour. When the draw for the order of play was made in an impressive ceremony at the Hotel de Ville, it was announced that the French would use, as their second singles player behind Henri Cochet, a talented and rising 19-year-old, Andre Merlin. In private the British team was delighted with the decision, suspecting that despite his enormous promise Merlin would struggle to cope with the pressure of making his Davis Cup debut in the Challenge Round.

This hunch was borne out when in the opening rubber Bunny Austin beat Merlin in straight sets to put the British ahead. In the stifling heat of a late July afternoon, Perry next had to take on Cochet, who 'let's face it, was my idol', and who had prevailed in the decisive match in the Challenge Round two years earlier. It was a tough and tense encounter from the start. Perry served several double faults and rushed too many shots in losing a long first set 10-8; he then played more steadily to take the next two. When a resurgent Cochet took the fourth set, a barnstorming finish looked on the cards. But instead, as Wallis Myers wrote in the *Telegraph*, 'Cochet had shot his bolt.'[6] As against Vines the previous week, Perry's superior fitness was now starting to pay dividends: he took the final set 6-1.

Jubilation in the British camp contrasted with booing from sections of the crowd as the players made their way off court, but it soon became clear that Perry's victory came at a price. Pushed to the limits in the stifling heat, Perry passed out in the dressing room, and after coming round he was initially unable to recall who had won the match. Being caught up in all the emotion of beating Cochet and avenging the defeat of 1931 had led to both mental and physical exhaustion. Roper Barrett swore the team to secrecy lest news of Perry's difficulty gave renewed encouragement to the French.

After a night's sleep Perry still seemed subdued by his standards, and the captain decided that – in order to save him for a possible decisive singles on the last day – he would use Harold Lee in his place in the doubles. Pat Hughes, Perry's usual partner, was far from happy with this decision, feeling he and Lee had no time to prepare adequately. These fears were borne out when the British pair were easily seen off by Borotra and Brugnon, ensuring the tie and the destiny of the trophy was still in the balance going into the final day.

The large solid silver Davis Cup was prominently on display as the French sought to make one last effort to reach a record-equalling seventh consecutive win. Cochet, proving remarkably resilient after his loss on the first day, refused to surrender in a pulsating clash with Austin and eventually came through in five sets. Once again Perry was in the spotlight in the deciding rubber.

Any British hopes that he would easily crush his inexperienced opponent disappeared as Merlin took the first set 6-4. Perry took the next two sets, but a ten-minute break allowed the Frenchman to regroup for strong resistance in the fourth. The tension was almost unbearable as Perry dropped his serve at 5-4 up. He broke Merlin again for a 6-5 advantage, and as the players changed ends, Roper Barrett decided to try something different. As he accompanied his player to the other side of the net he said to Perry that if he won the next game he would secure him a date with an attractive girl sitting in the crowd. In his memoirs Perry claimed this technique 'did the trick' – he closed out the match 7-5.[7]

It wasn't clear if Perry got the date with the girl, but he certainly got the plaudits for securing a famous victory. As Maskell observed, 'We had done it! At last, after a gap of 21 years, Britain had once more won the Davis Cup. The scenes on court were unforgettable. Perry was swamped in a sea of well-wishers.' It was Fred's iron concentration, Maskell said, that won the day.

After the official dinner later in the evening, Cochet – swallowing national pride – suggested the teams go out for a night on the town, and it was not until 7am that they returned to the hotel after visiting several hostelries and clubs. Suffering from the effects of the celebrations, the return journey to Britain proved arduous. Bunny Austin recalled that the team came across the Channel in a gale 'that turned us green'.[8]

All of this was forgotten when the squad received a congratulations message from the King at Dover and then travelled on by train to Victoria, where a crowd estimated at over 5,000 had gathered to give the victors a warm, noisy reception. The numbers were so great that mounted police had to clear a way for the players to get through the crowds.

There could be no doubt that the British team struck an emotional chord in scaling the heights of world tennis for the first time since 1912. For several days to come the players were inundated with phone calls of congratulation and requests for interviews and photographs, and all were given gold watches at an LTA banquet held in their honour at the Savoy hotel.

For all members of the team it was to be a major highlight in their careers. But for Perry especially it was a hugely significant moment. He had not only been rewarded for his steadfast loyalty to the cause, having played in all 17 ties played by the British team since he joined it three years earlier. He had also finally demolished the notion that he always buckled when push came to shove, as he had against Germany in 1932 and against France before that in 1931. Far from being a 'derelict old cab horse', he had forced his critics to eat their words. 'To Perry every praise,' wrote Wallis Myers. He had proved himself 'staunch and steady... A man less resolute might easily have surrendered to the physical and psychological forces opposed to him'.[9]

The new-style Perry training regime was now paying dividends in the sport's greatest team event, though as it turned out, he was still reliant on providence to help propel him to the very pinnacle of the individual game.

7

American and Australian champion

FRED PERRY rarely lacked belief in his own ability. Many observers felt he was something of a poseur on court, and even admirers agreed his plain speaking earned him a reputation for arrogance. He was once heard to say upon entering the dressing room ahead of a match, 'Thank God I'm not playing me today.'

Winning the Davis Cup had the effect of further bolstering Perry's self-assurance, and it was small wonder he regarded this as the time when his career really blossomed. Having secured the major prize in team tennis in the most testing of circumstances, he was able to banish any lingering doubts in his own mind about shortcomings in his individual game. It was with renewed vigour that in the months after the Davis Cup Final he moved towards becoming the world's best singles player. It was no coincidence that the big breakthrough moments came not in Britain but a long way from home, in the United States and in Australia, where Perry was not the subject of what he felt was the stifling, disapproving attention of the tennis authorities. Reinforced self-confidence did not, however, tell the whole story of what happened next: lady luck was about to intervene again.

The most important individual triumph of Perry's career to date came at the American national championships in September 1933. He arrived for his fourth visit to the USA still suffering from the draining effects of the tie against France, so much so that the LTA permitted him to avoid playing singles in the run-up to the championships.

From his previous visits Perry was already a well-known figure in New York, and with his status enhanced further by the Davis Cup victory, he was soon being spoken of as one of the favourites – along with Crawford and Vines – to take the American title. This heightened interest led to the first bout of speculation that was to grow and dominate Perry's career over the next couple of years.

Even though he was yet to win a major tournament, questions were asked about whether he intended to turn professional; the 'newshounds' started to follow him everywhere.[1] At this point he politely rebutted any suggestions that he might be leaving the amateur game, though the same could not be said of one of his major rivals: Ellsworth Vines.

For some time it had been an open secret that Vines was preparing to join Tilden in becoming a touring professional. Tilden first made overtures in 1931, conscious that Vines was desperately in need of income to support the mother who sacrificed so much for him in his early days and also a young wife. Negotiations to facilitate a switch to pro tennis unsettled Vines, helping to explain a poor run of form in 1933 that culminated in his early exit at Forest Hills. This, arguably, was the third time (following the Perry family move to the heartland of the English game and Sam Perry's unprompted willingness to support his son financially in 1930) that providence intervened in a crucial way to smooth Fred's path to domination of the men's game.

From their earliest encounters, Vines always seemed to come out on top, hitting with such force that the Englishman was regularly outgunned. 'There was only one way to beat Perry,' Vines later wrote. 'Overpower him.'[2] With the departure of the American, aged only 22 – he made his professional debut against Tilden at Madison Square Garden in January 1934 – the chances of Perry forcing his way to the pinnacle of the amateur game were significantly increased.

It was likely, even had Vines remained in the amateur game, that Perry's qualities would have seen him become a grand slam champion in the not too distant future.

But whether he would have dominated in the mid-1930s to the extent he did remains open to question. In their later encounters as professionals, as much as in their amateur days, Vines retained the upper hand. The central importance of the 'Vines factor' was evident even before the Californian signed his pro contract. Vines was in the same section of the draw as Perry at Forest Hills, and his unexpectedly early defeat not only dashed his hopes of leaving the amateur ranks in style, but also left the Englishman with a relatively straightforward path to the final. This he grasped with straight-sets wins over the Australian Quist in the quarter-final and the American Stoefen in the semis.

In the final Perry came up against the redoubtable Jack Crawford, seeking to become the first man to take all four major titles in the same year. Yet Fred was far from overawed by the prospect. Crawford's style of play contained little of the raw power and aggression that he found so difficult to contain in Vines. Perry had less to lose as the underdog, and he was enjoying every minute of the attention that came with his rising status.

Rex Bellamy, tennis correspondent of *The Times*, later observed that Fred possessed a 'nature that is in harmony with the bustling tempo of New York'.[3] As an illustration of the point, Perry accepted an offer from one of his growing band of American friends, a sheriff of the district in which Forest Hills was situated, to provide him with a police escort to the tournament. He turned up in a Rolls-Royce, preceded by four motorcycle policemen, in a flamboyant display the like of which the authorities would not have tolerated in Britain.

Whereas Perry went on court for the final more at ease than in his homeland and ready to strut, Crawford was a pale shadow of the figure who dominated over the previous nine months. On a typically humid New York day, with a gusty wind also blowing, Crawford was suffering from the effects of asthma and insomnia, having hardly slept at all during his two weeks at the tournament. The last thing he wanted was a protracted final, but this was what he got as the match developed into a titanic struggle. Perry took the first set and it required an enormous effort by Crawford to take the next two; the second set especially was draining for both men before it was won 13-11.

Ever alert to a possible psychological advantage, Perry used the ten-minute break at the end of the third set to change and reappear in fresh, pressed clothing, while Crawford sat court-side smoking a cigarette. Whether the effect was as intended or not, Perry seized the initiative, sweeping through the last two sets for the loss of only one game. The Australian was denied the place in the history books that would have been his had he captured all four grand slams in the same year. 'It was not particularly to my credit,' Perry wrote in generous vein afterwards. 'Everything came off for me! Everything failed for him!'4

It was a superbly satisfying achievement for Perry, making him the first British player to win the American title in 30 years. Although not obvious at the time, it marked a decisive shift in the balance of power. 'Gentleman Jack' was to win only one more major title, while for Perry it represented the start of three full years of ascendancy; a period when he reached every grand slam singles final in which he competed except on a couple of occasions when injury affected his performance. Among the many telegrams he received after the final one came from the Los Angeles club in California, offering him congratulations on continuing the tradition of Pacific Southwest winners going on to triumph at Forest Hills. Another was from Bunny Austin, and read simply, 'Well done, old cab horse.'

Perry decided it was time to let his hair down, as a New York journalist discovered when he sought out the title-holder. Arriving at the Madison for an interview, the journalist eventually found the new champion 'on the roof surrounded by pretty girls and an Hawaiian band. The life of an international tennis star seems to have its points.'

Having snatched such an important prize, Perry resolved not to attach too much importance to his tennis as he embarked on the long route to California. But riding on the crest of a wave he managed to retain his Pacific title, prompting the tournament secretary Perry Jones to declare that this made him a certainty for the US crown again in 1934. The exertions of the autumn did have some adverse effects. Perry and Crawford, both exhausted, were doing no more than go through the motions in an exhibition match at the Los Angeles club when Marlene Dietrich, hostess for the occasion, suddenly said, 'Well, gentlemen, I think you could at least *try*.'[5]

From San Francisco, Perry sailed west across the Pacific for a new adventure at the end of 1933. The LTA had earlier decided to send a British team to Australia, where a series of 'test matches' were organised in part to smooth over relations strained by the controversial Bodyline cricket tour the previous winter. After what he called a glorious maiden cross-Pacific voyage, with stops in Tahiti and New Zealand, Perry was immediately struck by the easy-going, hospitable ways of his Australian hosts.

There was some lingering resentment towards the English cricket team, and Perry soon began making friends and doing his bit for improved diplomatic relations. He warmed to both the people and the country, which struck him as having many similarities with the United States. Among the highlights of the visit were a first experience of flying, travelling round the country for the test matches in what he called 'a boneshaker with two wings and a prayer', and a trip to the outback, which included the traditional Aussie pastime of hunting kangaroos. Although he raised his gun in readiness to shoot, the kangaroo in his sights looked him straight in the eye, and he was unable to pull the trigger.[6]

Despite the Australians prevailing in the team-based matches, Perry was determined to prove himself in the individual tournaments that formed part of the tour. Many leading amateurs could ill afford the time or the money required to spend weeks travelling by boat to Australia from Europe or the United States. The number of quality performers at the Australian Championships was consequently less than at other grand slam events, though the Aussies were known for being resolute opponents on their home territory.

Perry defeated Crawford to win one of the warm-up events, the Victorian Championships held in Melbourne, and by the time he reached Sydney for the national championships, held at Rushcutters Bay in late January 1934, he was hitting peak form. *The Times* reported that Perry showed his unique fitness by playing nine sets in the searing sun on a single day, though the ultra-fast grass courts at least made for short rallies. After losing the first two sets to Vivian McGrath in the semi-final of the singles, he found his range on his forehand drives and gradually seized the initiative.

In the final set, 'Perry's experience told its tale. He served brilliantly, and won with the loss of only one game.'[7] He then went back on to court with Pat Hughes to secure the doubles title with a four-set win over the Australians Quist and Turnbull, so repeating their victory over the same pair in the Davis Cup the previous year.

On 27 January, in front of an 8,000-strong crowd, Perry secured the victory he set his heart on, keen to show that his triumph at Forest Hills was not a flash in the pan. He defeated 'Gentleman Jack' for the third time in succession, this time on Crawford's home patch. Despite the exertions of the previous day (when Crawford won his semi quickly in contrast to Perry's lengthy toils), it was also by the most comfortable margin yet, in three straight sets. Crawford served poorly at the outset, and while the second set proved tight, Perry pulled away to win emphatically in the third. Much of the game was played from the baseline, with Perry hustling Crawford's backhand in particular to force errors. Although disappointed to see the three-time Australian champion beaten, the home spectators gave Perry a great ovation as he left the court: a sign that his on-court persona was primarily an issue at home in Britain. In the days that followed Fred received widespread, if restrained, plaudits in the British press. The *Manchester Guardian* wrote that his triumph might do much 'to explode the popular fallacy that England had deteriorated athletically'.[8]

Perry was frequently asked in the aftermath of his second grand slam victory why, for some months past, he appeared to have finally got the measure of his Australian adversary. His response was to talk of a difference in stamina, alluding not only to his own improved fitness but also accepting that Crawford was tired from earlier exertions.

In addition he referred – with typical attention to detail – to watching film material of a previous encounter with Crawford that alerted him to the need to work extra hard on his service returns. Only much later, in his 1984 autobiography, did he also mention the fact that Vines was no longer in contention. Against Crawford, he was quite happy to trade shots from the baseline, awaiting the right opportunity to attack. Crawford (as well as Austin and von Cramm) did not hit with sufficient power to embarrass him regularly from the baseline. By contrast Perry picked out Vines, plus the more unpredictable Czech Menzel, as someone who could blast winners from any part of the court.

In February there were further test matches to complete – though the 'snap rather left the tour' after the national championships, as Perry put it – before he set sail for England on a P&O liner. By the time he arrived home in mid-March 1934 he had been away for eight months and had travelled an estimated 9,000 miles by steamship, rail, aircraft and motor car. As soon as he arrived in London he was being pestered with the question: as champion of both America and Australia, would he be turning professional?

In his memoirs he recalled his response at this point was to say he was not even interested; his over-riding priority after winning two major titles was to capture the greatest of them all, in London SW19. While his answer was sincere, he was undoubtedly sympathetic towards professionalism, and had already been made a substantial financial offer to join Tilden's pro circuit.[9]

Back at his family home in Ealing, life had changed significantly. In 1931 Sam Perry, a year or so after the death of his first wife, married Olive Gardner, a secretary at the Co-op party headquarters. Fred it appears was still grieving the loss of his mother, and had few dealings with Sam's new wife (who was only a few years his senior), though she did help in typing up the manuscript of a book he produced in conjunction with the *London Evening Standard* journalist Bruce Harris.

My Story, a work of 'reminiscences, experiences, and impressions' was penned in the spring and published in the summer of 1934. While much of the book was made up of accounts of his rise through the ranks, together with practical tips for club players, a whole chapter was devoted to a topic that was gaining ever more prominence in his mind, 'The Case for Professionalism'. This was topical at the time as the sport's global authority, the ILTF, had recently attacked 'shamateurism': under-the-counter abuses of the amateur rules, though it did introduce at the discretion of individual national governing bodies an 'eight-weeks rule', allowing a set level of expenses for what it felt was a reasonable period of play in any one year.[10]

It was clear from the chapter in *My Story* where Perry's sympathies lay. Although he held back from biting the hand that fed him, acknowledging the great support the LTA had provided, much of the wording was easy to interpret as a veiled attack on amateurism. Younger players, he said, often discussed the rules governing the sport in dressing rooms and hotels – probably more so after the exit of Vines from the amateur game – and Perry's viewpoint was heavily underscored by his personal experiences. The reality, he argued, was that it was becoming impossible to combine regular salaried employment with serious competition at the highest level in world tennis.

On this he firmly if cautiously criticised the governing bodies, noting that they were happy to encourage the growth of tennis as a global enterprise, yet stuck with amateur rules that made it difficult for anyone except those with wealth and leisure to compete. Unless a player, he said, had a very sympathetic employer, they had little chance of reaching the top; the European tennis calendar alone stretched from May to July.

At the heart of the issue was the insistence of the amateur authorities that tennis should be played for pleasure not profit, and it was on this that feelings were most impassioned. Top players, Perry noted, gain from the game 'every material advantage *except money*', even though money is paid by the public to see them perform and they know that their careers will be short. While at pains to stress that he enjoyed his tennis and travels to the full, Perry saw nothing inherently wrong with the course prominent amateurs such as Tilden (and subsequently Frenchman Cochet as well as Vines) had taken.

There had, he claimed, been much 'loose talk' in the press about shamateurs, those who were alleged to gain huge sums from under-the-counter sources. But he knew of no one who had become a millionaire by such means. In terms of his own financial position, Perry conceded he was able, without breaching amateur rules, to make small sums from his writing for London newspapers. But this represented his sole source of private income, and while on his travels around the world his home governing body was he noted 'strict in enforcing its rules about expenses'.[11]

Indeed, unlike many associations overseas, the LTA took such a hard line that it opted out of implementing the eight weeks' rule accepted by the ILTF, feeling it would be difficult to police and the thin end of a wedge leading to unlimited expenses for top amateurs.

At this critical juncture in his career, having returned triumphant from a long tour abroad, Perry was thus well-apprised of the dilemma facing the world's elite players, one that was to loom ever larger in his mind over the next couple of years. Reading between the lines of his 1934 book it was readily apparent in which direction he was moving. He refused to follow the example of many in the amateur tennis establishment who condemned top players like Vines for choosing professionalism.

With no background or training like other senior British players in banking or commerce, he did not have a ready-made career to turn to once his playing days were finished, and if he found life at home in Ealing less congenial after the death of his mother then he would inevitably be thinking about where he might live and how he might finance himself in the longer term. He knew however that to cash in on his talent at this point, following the path trailed by Tilden, would mean early exile from the amateur game, and so for the time being his priority remained to consolidate his place at the top of the men's game.

In 1933, Jack Crawford was indisputably the world number one, having captured three of the four major titles. But from the autumn onwards, going into the early months of 1934, Perry beat Crawford three times in succession in five-set matches, suffering just one reverse in a three-set encounter.

As a column attributed to 'The Bystander' in the magazine *Lawn Tennis and Badminton* noted in March 1934, this record was such that Perry should be hailed as the top amateur in the world. 'We seem to be accepting the fact very quietly.' The Bystander added, 'if Perry were an American his name would be stuck up in the newspaper headlines far more frequently than it is in England.'[12]

In spite of the advances he had made since the previous summer, helping to secure British victory in the Davis Cup and seizing the American and Australian titles, Perry had still not captured the hearts and minds of the British tennis public. His achievements had all come overseas, in Paris, New York and Sydney. The paradox was that at the time of his 25th birthday, in May 1934, Fred Perry was an international star, feted at tennis venues round the globe, but he remained somewhat underappreciated in Britain. He knew he would remain so unless he could triumph in his own backyard at the cradle of lawn tennis – Wimbledon.

8

World number one

MOST tennis observers in Britain knew little of the new, improved Fred Perry who returned home after eight months away in the spring of 1934. Few British journalists had been present in New York or Australia to witness the extent to which he had remedied past shortcomings, notably his habit of relinquishing matches from winning positions. Those who continued to harbour doubts were given fresh ammunition when he failed at the first major of the European playing season – the French Championships in May.

All was going well as Perry swept into the quarter-finals, beating en route the likes of his French Davis Cup adversary Andre Merlin without dropping a set. But he next came up against the ambidextrous Italian Giorgio de Stefani, who knocked him out of the same event in

1931. *The Times* reported that in the process of losing by three sets to one, Perry, 'whose chances of winning the championships were thought much of', suffered an ankle injury when stretching for a return. He finished out the match 'pluckily', rather than conceding. But the injury looked severe, 'As he limped forward to congratulate the winner he collapsed and was carried off court.'[1]

According to Perry in his 1984 memoirs, he offered to give his opponent an honourable victory on the condition that de Stefani did not run him ragged in the process. But the Italian was not in a charitable mood (any more, it must be said, than Perry tended to be in matches when he was in the ascendant), and he forced the Englishman to run to the corners as he harried him to defeat. Perry was enraged and threatened revenge as he left the court, though past experience showed the redoubtable Italian was always hard to beat on clay.

This story may have been embellished for effect – especially after Fred humiliated his opponent in a later match on grass – for after the match Perry made no reference to a 'pact' and only spoke of de Stefani's considerateness in not making things worse for the injured ankle. For sceptics and doubters, it was easy enough to conclude this was the Perry of old, falling short before reaching the final hurdle.

With hindsight, the defeat in Paris turned out to be the only setback that prevented Perry from going into the history books as the first winner of all the grand slam events in the same calendar year. But at the time, the ankle injury lowered expectations about what Perry might achieve in London SW19.

He was out of action for a few weeks, and despite expert medical attention there were rumours he was still moving gingerly when the tournament began. In reality, Fred had come through some tough warm-up sets with Dan Maskell, and as play got under way he remained healthy while several rivals suffered from freak fitness problems.

The 1934 Championships were blessed with fine and sunny weather throughout, conditions that may have been linked with a mysterious malady soon dubbed by the press the 'Wimbledon throat'. In the first week this forced over 50 competitors to retire and left others performing well below their best. The cause of the players' malaise was not immediately apparent. The Water Board prohibited the watering of lawns in the area owing to the dry conditions, and it was only later concluded that the problem was most likely due to a film of crystals over the courts resulting from the use of an emergency water supply.

Unlike Jack Crawford, Perry – seeded behind the defending champion at number two – was not affected in any way by the 'throat', though he was still not moving with his customary fluency in the first couple of rounds, where he eased past Raymond Tuckey (the only British opponent he faced in the three years of his Wimbledon ascendancy) and the American veteran Dick Williams. Although it took five hard sets to beat the dangerous, unpredictable Czech player Roderick Menzel and the American Sidney Wood in the semi-final, Perry had put the injury behind him and looked supremely confident as he went out on Centre Court for his first appearance in the final on 6 July.

Fred Burrow's view of the rout that followed was that the Englishman was a revelation. Everyone knew of his record since the summer of 1933. Even so, 'We did not know Perry then... the Wimbledon public had never seen him at his best. That Friday he showed them. There was no flaw at all in his game, he didn't make a dozen poor shots in the whole match.'[2]

Among the first to congratulate the new Wimbledon champion – the person who along with his mentor Pops Summers felt most proud and vindicated – was his father. Although Sam Perry was no longer an MP, he devoted considerable energy to touring the country making speeches in an effort to help revive Labour after its shattering election defeat in 1931. But he still had more time than in earlier years to watch his son compete, and was a frequent spectator at Wimbledon.

As he came down from the stands to greet Fred coming off court after securing the title, he was in tears, as was Maskell. While a few friends and family were overcome with emotion, Perry was soon made aware that others were not so moved. After the unceremonious draping of the All England Club tie over his chair in the dressing room, his mood changed from joy to fury. 'That stuck-up attitude hurt, it really did', he wrote in his memoirs.

He realised that for the tennis establishment there was a clear distinction between doing well in the Davis Cup, being part of a victorious team, and winning the affections of fans on the basis of individual accomplishments. The new champion called for the LTA secretary Anthony Sabelli, whom he regarded as one of his few allies in the hierarchy, and told him he would not play in Britain's forthcoming Challenge Round encounter with the United States unless he received an apology for the alleged comment that 'the best man' had not triumphed.[3]

Jon Henderson argues that, if for Wimbledon insiders and followers, Perry was perversely 'more admired than loved', he was 'held in high esteem by the vast majority of the nation'. Although there were other individual sporting successes to celebrate in 1934, notably with Henry Cotton triumphing at golf's Open Championship, Henderson claims that Fred's victory at Wimbledon – part of a period in which he went unbeaten in over 20 matches at the Championships – brought him to 'a place in the estimation of the British public that was probably as exalted as any domestic sportsman or woman has achieved'.[4]

Yet the manner in which Perry was perceived by the sporting and wider public may be best described as complex and multi-layered, and can only be understood with reference to how he presented himself and the way in which tennis was reported by the media in the 1930s. Ted Tinling, whose role at Wimbledon at the time was to accompany the players from the changing rooms on to court, astutely reflected on how Perry was not good at communicating with home fans, adding that had he done so he would have increased his popularity.

In practice, connecting with the sporting public was not easy in an age when there were few agents or experts to help mould players' images. If he was to reach out more successfully than hitherto to the Wimbledon crowds and wider opinion, Perry would have to do so largely under his own steam. His profile was of course considerably raised after 1934 as a constant stream of journalists wanted to question the latest winner of the world's most renowned tournament.

But if this brought him to the wider attention of the middle-class readers of broadsheets such as *The Times* and *Telegraph*, these traditionalist papers were adamant that sporting success should be greeted with decorum and should be placed in an appropriate perspective. An editorial commenting on the victories of Perry and Henry Cotton advised that, while welcome, it was important to remember that 'a game is a game'. Nor should it be forgotten that many of the tabloids usually gave little coverage to tennis, regarded in the 1930s as a sport of peripheral concern to working-class readers.

While there were countless newsreel clips of Perry, ensuring his face became recognisable across the globe, this was a long way from the cult of sporting celebrity that developed with the coming of television after the Second World War. Perry's reputation at home, and his legacy in terms of galvanising British tennis, might have been different had he become familiar through the emerging medium of TV. As a natural in front of the cameras, it was ironic that his amateur career was to end just when the BBC was first experimenting with televised coverage of the Championships in 1937. The experiment was so successful that it was decided to extend Wimbledon coverage in the final years before the outbreak of war, though by 1939 only around 2,000 TV sets had been sold in Britain.[5]

In Perry's prime playing days radio therefore remained central to media coverage of sport, with some eight million licences in circulation. Soon after the BBC established itself as a public-service broadcaster in 1927, the AEC accepted a request to transmit commentaries of important matches at the Championships. By the early 1930s Wimbledon was firmly established as part of the BBC's portfolio of sports coverage, and Perry thereby secured wide exposure via the airwaves.

This did not automatically ensure, however, that his appeal across classes was broadened. In the view of the historian Mike Huggins, 'BBC radio, a major cultural force, pursued middle-brow culture and taste in difficult times by largely transmitting a middle-class vision of British sport, a vision which also shaped BBC commentaries.'

Radio presenters were usually public school and university educated, and commentary tended to be sympathetic to the norms of gentlemanly amateurism, as well as using standard English in ways that were sometimes off-putting to working-class audiences. The speech patterns of those employed to cover the Championships, such as the ex-Wimbledon umpire, Captain H.B.T. 'Teddy' Wakelam, meant the name of the nation's best player was usually pronounced 'Perrae'. The public, as a result, were not encouraged to get too carried away about their new champion. As Huggins writes, this was a distinctly British style of commentary, 'Unlike American broadcasts, there was rarely exaggeration, over-dramatisation or over-excitement.'[6]

Despite his pre-eminence in the summer of 1934, the reality was that a vast social gulf continued to exist between Perry and the majority of those who played, administered, watched or listened to tennis in Britain. Appealing to those involved in the sport was almost second nature for gentleman amateurs such as Jack Crawford. The warm applause he received in losing to Perry suggested that many spectators concurred with the idea (whether it was articulated in the dressing room or not) of Crawford as the 'best man', wording that conveyed something other than the 'best player'. The unassuming

Australian gave the impression of being a genial country squire; he used an old-style square-topped racquet and always wore traditional flannel cricket shirts with long sleeves. He was also associated with polite court manners, and with a habit of drinking from a pot of tea at end changes in long matches.

The sympathies of the Wimbledon faithful could be won over by those from modest backgrounds, but only if the game was played in what was believed to be the right spirit. Dorothy Round's victory in the women's singles the day after the men's final was followed by a rapturous reception from the crowd, yet her family history bore some similarities to that of Perry. Surveying the scene on Centre Court, Davis Cup captain Roper Barrett said to Tinling, 'Fred could have had all this yesterday, if only he'd let them understand him.' The key consideration, Tinling believed, was that Miss Round was widely regarded as charming, modest and deferential. This he felt explained why her victory roused spectators to 'fever pitch', whereas, 'Fred's achievement had been greeted with only cool acknowledgement.'[7]

It would be misleading to imply that Perry's sole reaction to winning Wimbledon was a sense of being undervalued. He loved the tournament and the venue from the time he first went there, and he tried hard to put behind him the dressing room incident and his clashes with one or two establishment figures. There were certainly numerous experiences to cherish and enjoy in the days after the final against Crawford. He was enormously touched by the warmth of the crowd when he and Dorothy Round made their bows in the royal box at the end of the Championships.

Much to his delight, Fred was given a civic reception at Ealing town hall, after which he was carried shoulder high by members of the Brentham tennis club to his car. He was also pleased to be made a guest of honour, together with Dorothy Round, at the annual banquet of the LTA held at the Savoy hotel. Perry and Miss Round were met with prolonged cheers from the 300 guests as they made their way to the top table. The president of the LTA, the Conservative minister Sir Samuel Hoare, congratulated Perry on his brilliant victory, and in a gracious reply the new champion admitted that luck had been on his side throughout, from being spared the effects of the 'Wimbledon throat' to taking the title on a double fault. He was, he said, 'naturally very pleased and proud to bring back the Championship to England after so many years'.[8]

The match in which Perry threatened not to participate, the Davis Cup tie against the United States, in the event passed off smoothly. Placated by the apology he received for what went on in the dressing room after the Wimbledon final, Fred – despite some concern over soreness in his back – played a key role in helping Britain to retain the trophy. As holders, the British team was in the enviable position of not needing to play until the Challenge Round.

Instead of enduring several high-pressure ties as in previous years, Perry joined his team-mates practising in a leisurely fashion on the grass at Devonshire Park in Eastbourne. When the time came to take on the Americans in late July, both Perry and Austin were relaxed and ready. The two British players won both of their singles, against Sidney Wood and Frank Shields. Although the doubles was lost, Britain eased to a 4-1 success, retaining the Davis Cup without the final-rubber drama experienced when it was captured in Paris.

In what proved to be the decisive encounter, Perry recalled that his match with Shields provoked the 17,000-strong crowd into 'a most un-Wimbledon-like state of frenzy and disorder', with the umpire frequently having to call for quiet.[9]

The excitement in the stands as the tie reached its climax did not necessarily signal a sudden sea-change in attitudes towards Perry once his reputation was established beyond all doubt as Wimbledon champion. It was perhaps more to do with the team setting of Davis Cup play, which encouraged noisy patriotic support; and it may also have reflected the fact that Perry and Shields were regarded as the two most handsome men in the game.

Shields, born the same year as Perry in the Bronx, was a playboy well known in American high society, a free spirit who travelled the amateur circuit looking for amorous adventure, rather than with a burning desire to be the best. According to the biography written by his son, while Frank was a keen competitor, after any match – win or lose – he 'took a shower and looked forward to the evening'. At the end of 1934, when playing in California, a film executive offered Shields a lucrative movie contract after noticing how schoolgirls watching him play were almost uncontrollable with excitement.[10]

Perry was capable of making a similar impression, and this points to another side of the coin in terms of his public persona. While his background and attitudes did not go down well among the senior figures (always men) who administered British tennis, he was unquestionably attractive to large numbers of women, especially those who followed the game casually from afar, whether in newspapers or catching glimpses of him in newsreels.

Like Shields, Perry was a dashing figure with a powerful physique, dark features and sleek hair; he also was popular in Hollywood, which more than anything else helped to provide him with a glamorous image. Ted Tinling said of Fred that women were 'more attracted by his obvious virility than touched by his lack of traditional sportsmanlike demeanour'. Alan Trengrove, chronicler of the Davis Cup, believed this was particularly noticeable in team events when crowds felt freer to express their emotions, 'When Perry walked out to play in his crisp white flannels and matching white blazer, thousands of female hearts missed a beat.'[11]

Within weeks of the Davis Cup success, Perry was on his travels again as he set off to the USA to defend his title at Forest Hills. He looked to be in imperious form as he progressed to the final, mostly at the expense of lesser-known American players, dropping only one set in the process. As the overwhelming favourite, and having not been pushed hard, complacency and rustiness may have been at work when he almost let slip his title.

For the first time in a while he allowed himself to be pegged back from a 2-0 sets lead in the final against Wilmer Allison. Pulling himself together in the decider, he managed to sneak home 8-6, reverting to what he felt were the best tactics to counter Allison's strong volleying game: pinning him back as far as possible to the baseline. Although not at his most fluent, this second American Championship confirmed Perry as the world's best.

He had won three major titles since the turn of the year, and his only grand slam setback – in Paris – owed much to injury. None of his main rivals seemed to have any answer either to his early-ball game or to the air of certainty he exuded on and off court.

One American writer claimed that after defending his US title the 'cocky Britisher' rushed back to the Madison, his New York hotel, expecting the clerks to laugh at the same joke he made the previous year, 'Has the King called yet to congratulate me?'[12]

Victory at Forest Hill made it inevitable that, having climbed to number two in 1933, Perry finally reached the top spot in the 'World's First Ten' for 1934 (with Jack Crawford second), a position he was to retain for the next two years.

Having even featured on the front of *Time* magazine, Fred the international tennis star was on the crest of a wave at the close of 1934. But this did not tell the whole story of how he was feeling off court.

If there was a period when Perry enjoyed in an entirely uncomplicated way his number one status – itself questionable, in view of what happened in the dressing room after his Wimbledon victory – then it was short-lived. Now that he was a grand slam champion three times over, in Australia and the US as well as at Wimbledon, the press were constantly quizzing him about whether he might leave amateur tennis.

Especially when he was in North America, where pro tennis had a foothold, the questioning seemed to grow ever more nagging wherever he went. From the autumn of 1934 onward, interrogations of Fred about his future dogged him relentlessly, and on occasion were to seriously affect his performance on court. The trickle of interest in his playing status was turning into a torrent.

9

On the brink

IN 1935 Perry moved to the brink of deciding he would turn professional. Throughout the year his status as world number one was never seriously in doubt. But for much of the time he was struggling with conflicting emotions, on and off court. In an age, unlike today, when tennis stars could not count on entourages of travelling coaches and assistants, they had to deal personally with the various demands placed upon them: in particular by governing bodies, over matters such as expenses, and by the press, ever eager to find copy to fill newspapers.

With only a few close confidants such as his father and Pops Summers to call upon – and these often thousands of miles away in Britain while he travelled the world – Fred struggled to come to terms with the extra attention accorded to the world's best player. As a result he went through a topsy-turvy season in which he experienced numerous highs and lows. He tasted both continued success and bitter defeat on court, while in his private life he took the huge step of marrying after first calling off an earlier engagement.

Much of the pressure he felt under came from relentless probing by journalists, which now had a twin focus: on the international celebrity who fraternised with Hollywood actresses, and on the champion who was flirting with the option of leaving the amateur game.

If Perry hoped an announcement in late 1934 that he intended for the time being to remain an amateur ('so that I could play for Great Britain') would settle the matter, he was quickly disabused. As he made his way across the Pacific with a view to defending his Australian title after Christmas, his ship was frequently radioed for information and he was pestered at every landfall. In New Zealand he was even questioned by a journalist who sat next to him as he tried to relax watching a film at the cinema.

Once he arrived in Australia the same pattern continued. Nobody seemed much interested in his tennis, only in the question of whether he might turn pro. There were signs the incessant probing contributed to a dip in form. With no agent or adviser close at hand, the Wimbledon and US champion had to take it on the chin when journalists pressed him over some poor showings in warm-up events, including defeat to Adrian Quist in the Victorian Championships.

At the Australian national championships in Melbourne in January 1935, it looked as if Perry was back in the groove. In the quarter-final he exacted revenge on Giorgio de Stefani for his defeat in Paris the previous spring, inflicting in the process one of the most crushing defeats ever in the last eight of a major tournament (without the loss of a single game). The Englishman was in similarly good touch when he beat Vivian McGrath in the semi-finals for the loss of just six games in three sets.

According to *The Times*, Jack Crawford would need to be in exceptionally good form if he was to upset the odds in the final.[1] In the event, Crawford did not play brilliantly, but well enough to stem his run of reverses against Perry. As a spectacle the match suffered because both men played defensively. Perry usually found his baseline game strong enough to overcome Crawford, but on this occasion he failed to change tactics as his error count rose in the face of the Australian's steady play. Part of the explanation for the outcome may have been complacency; Perry had grown accustomed to getting the better of Crawford.

But another reason why the Englishman lacked the energy or inclination to at least attempt to change the pattern of the game was later revealed. American promoters, he noted in his memoirs, had not given up hope of persuading him to turn professional in time for a winter tour in the United States. Talks rumbled on throughout the Australian Championships, and culminated in a dozen phone calls from London and the US the night before the final.[2]

In spite of the defeat in Australia – which potentially undercut what could be demanded of professional promoters – Fred continued to be dogged in the early months of 1935 by stories that he was about to quit amateur tennis. He wasn't helped in this regard by his travel arrangements. His long journey home to Britain went via California, where professionalism was more established than in Europe, with the result that journalists resumed their probing about his intentions. Perry responded with various non-committal replies, though the likes of Tilden and his associates got the impression that he was edging ever closer to coming on board the pro tour.

While Fred derived enormous pleasure from representing his country in the Davis Cup and winning top individual titles – all of which would have to be forsaken by turning pro – to set against this, he was coming close to having achieved all he could in the amateur game, and was ever more preoccupied with his long-term future.

Hence there was ambiguity in his public and private utterances, which included hints that he might move to base himself in the USA. It was certainly difficult to kill off rumours about his intentions at a time when, behind the scenes, he was made offers to make cameo appearances in Hollywood films.

Such appearances, Perry wrote in 1936, could have made him wealthy enough 'not to need to do another stroke of work'. He felt strongly that there would be no contravention of regulations about being paid for demonstrating individual tennis shots, but the ILTF ruled that if he went ahead, his amateur status would be revoked; a resolution that hardened his distrust of the authorities.[3]

Part of the reason Perry took the unusual decision to travel home from Australia via the USA in early 1935 was personal. His love life was becoming increasingly complicated. In August 1934 he announced his engagement to a young British actress, Mary Lawson, but with Fred away for a long stretch thereafter, the romance withered and the engagement was called off less than nine months later. In Hollywood rumours circulated of flings with well-known actresses such as Marlene Dietrich and before long it emerged that a serious relationship with a Hollywood actress was in the offing.

The object of Fred's affection was Helen Vinson, a Texan who had a contract with the Warner company. Vinson was 18 months older than Perry, tall and striking in appearance, and she featured in nearly 20 films in her first three years in Hollywood including *The Power and the Glory*. With a sultry low voice and a southern drawl, sometimes mistaken for an English accent, Vinson first met Perry on one of his earlier visits to California, and by 1935 the romance was blossoming.

When he finally arrived at Southampton in late April, Perry had to contend with a double distraction. As he stepped off the ship he was asked in front of the newsreel cameras about rumours that he intended to turn professional. He replied he would not do so 'yet awhile' and hoped to help keep the Davis Cup in England. Much of the focus of journalistic attention, however, came from the fact that as he stepped ashore he was accompanied by Helen Vinson, who needed to be in London to make a film. He later admitted it was difficult to concentrate on tennis with his girlfriend in close proximity.

He managed to retain his British Hard Court title at Bournemouth, though his preparation was far from ideal. It was not only in the United States that he faced intrusive enquiries about his future plans on an almost everyday basis.

And he was irked when he discovered that the LTA, despite all his recent success, would offer no more than two separate half hour slots when he requested practice time at Queen's Club to prepare for Bournemouth.

On the whole the signs were not promising when Perry made his way to Paris for the French Championships in May. Aside from the nagging questions about his future, he knew that clay was not his strongest surface. He had yet to put together a long string of wins at Roland Garros, going out at the quarter-final stage on each of his three previous visits. And so it was a surprise even to himself that he claimed the title in Paris.

Whether or not he benefited from the chance to escape from off-court pressures, Perry reasserted his domination over Crawford with a straight-sets win in the semi-finals, and in the final he played a patient game in overcoming one of Europe's finest clay court exponents, Gottfried von Cramm, 6-3, 3-6, 6-1, 6-3. *The Times* reported that both players allowed the tension of the occasion to inhibit their stroke play, and if Perry was not at his best, only occasionally coming to the net to volley, 'He at least made sure of a championship.'[4] In doing so he cemented a place for himself in the record books. He was not only the first British man to take the French title since the event was opened to non-French citizens and residents in 1925 (and remains the only one at the time of writing); he also became the first player to win all of the world's four grand slam events.

In contrast to the previous year, Wimbledon – on and off court – proved straightforward when Perry returned to defend his title in 1935.

Buoyed by his triumph in Paris, he went into the tournament certain in his mind that he would win; the defeat in Australia seemed a distant memory. He cruised to a succession of easy victories in the first week and, as in Paris, overcame first Crawford and then von Cramm to take the title. The German was a stylish player capable of high quality tennis, but having beaten him on clay in

Paris, Perry believed he would have little trouble on his preferred surface of grass.

He knew his opponent's long backswing made him prone to errors when hurried on grass, as well as making it easier to read the direction of his shots. In the cocksure way that grated with some, Perry told Duncan Macaulay on the morning of the final that he didn't really need his pre-arranged practice with Dan Maskell as he'd beat 'this fellow 6-2, 6-3, 6-4' – a prediction that proved to be only one game away from the actual score (6-4 in the second set). Watching court-side, Fred Burrow observed it was a well-deserved victory, secured by 'audacity, concentration, complete confidence…and that extra speed of foot and shot which no other player possesses'.[5]

To round off a successful fortnight, Perry also triumphed in an exciting mixed doubles final, teaming up with Dorothy Round to defeat the young Australian Harry Hopman and his wife.

The summer season ended on another high note at the end of July when the British team secured an emphatic 5-0 whitewash over the USA in the Challenge Round of the Davis Cup. Perry felt the Americans suffered from 'staleness'; this was the seventh time since 1927 they had contested and lost the Challenge Round.[6]

The crowds at Wimbledon were treated to an exciting first tie when Bunny Austin came within two points of defeat before beating Wilmer Allison. After this the momentum was firmly with the British team. Perry like

Austin won both his singles, defeating the net-rushing Allison and also 20-year-old Donald Budge, the young Californian emerging as a notable force in world tennis. In this first encounter, Perry was able to exploit Budge's inexperience to ease to a four-set victory.

An incident in the third set, with the scores even, illustrated how relaxed Perry was with his game following his victories at Paris and Wimbledon. Budge sent up a lob and as Perry prepared to smash he was distracted by a piece of paper fluttering on to court, and missed an easy kill. The Englishman caught the paper, looked at it and began to laugh, eliciting a chuckle from the crowd. He called his opponent over and asked him to look at the paper, which was completely blank. On one level Perry was simply acting as a showman, looking to please the crowd, though it was likely he was also sending a message to his young opponent about who was in charge. By the end of the tie Britain's place as the leading force on the international stage was again confirmed. It was the first time since the days of the Doherty brothers that the British had won the Davis Cup three times in a row.

The European summer season thus proved hugely rewarding for Perry. Aside from confirming him as by some distance the best player in the world, he became engaged to Helen Vinson, and it was in a positive frame of mind that he set off for New York in August looking to secure his third successive win in the American Championships. But across the Atlantic the mood changed. He was plagued from the outset by further irritating speculation about whether he would leave the amateur game. He admitted in his memoirs that his mind was moving more towards taking the plunge by joining the pro game.

This perhaps signals the decisive moment in time, during the autumn of 1935, when a change in playing status became probable rather than possible. Had the switch been made at this point, Perry would have been able to claim that he had won all the four major titles at least once, as well as helping Britain to a hat-trick of Davis Cup successes. It may have been that another triumph at Forest Hills would have been enough to finalise a decision, providing both a fitting climax to his amateur career and an ideal entry point into the professional game. North American promoters were pushing hard for a fresh face to add to the Tilden–Vines circuit, and Perry was the obvious contender, especially as his nationality would allow a new tour to be billed as a titanic Anglo-American clash.

But any plans that were being hatched were shelved when, despite being the overwhelming favourite, he was beaten in the semi-finals of the US Championships. Perry had not lost an important singles match since the Australian final at the beginning of the year, and injury clearly played a key part in his demise in New York. In the first set of his match against Wilmer Allison, Fred skidded on the greasy surface and fell on to his racket;

he was in great pain and it later transpired he had broken a rib. Reluctant to retire, the Englishman continued despite being unable to serve fluently or to hit overheads. His opponent, Perry wrote, had a pleasant afternoon dropping the ball short to draw Fred to the net before lobbing him to maximise the discomfort, using 'tactics which made me as mad as hell'.

Allison won comfortably, and went on to become the first American winner at Forest Hills since 1932. Although this was the sort of ruthless treatment he was prepared to dish out when the occasion arose, Perry came off court fuming. His mood darkened further when he heard Allison telling reporters he believed he had found the right formula for beating the Englishman. Perry held his counsel and did not complain to the press, though he was convinced it was the injury that explained his loss to a player he beat regularly, most recently in the Davis Cup just weeks earlier.[7]

The American Championships were followed by an important announcement, though this came not in Perry's playing status but in his personal life. Back at the Madison hotel, where the atmosphere was solemn, one of his friends came up with the idea that Fred and Helen should head off and get married. On the spur of the moment this seemed like a good idea. As Perry recounted, a small party set off for Harrison, about 30 miles from New York. A magistrate was prevailed upon to come to the local police station and conduct the marriage service shortly before midnight. The boldness of the move looked more questionable in the cold light of day. 'We married in haste and repented the same way,' Perry recalled. With both parties bound up in their respective careers and constantly on the move, it was to be 'what people in those days called "a Hollywood marriage", i.e. doomed to failure'.[8]

After the marriage ceremony the newly-weds packed up and made their way to California, where they honeymooned at leisure, especially as with a broken rib Perry had no prospect of playing in the Pacific Southwest tournament. Although the early weeks of the marriage went swimmingly, Fred was entering uncharted and unsettling territory. His enforced absence from the courts meant he was inexorably drawn more than ever into the tedious speculation about his future, and he was conscious that he now had a wife to consider when pondering the issues.

Heading off to Australia later in the autumn, having pledged to return there and hoping to regain the national title – having spent only a month or so with Helen, who remained behind to resume her career – brought little succour. While the voyage provided a measure of respite, Perry knew instinctively that he was far from fit. In his opening match in one of the warm-up events he narrowly scraped through a five-setter, but he was in agony by the end. He left soon afterwards without playing in the Australian Championships.

In spite of marriage, two major titles and his undisputed place at the top of the 'World's First Ten', Fred Perry consequently ended 1935 much as he started it: at a low ebb. For such an all-action figure, prolonged absence through injury was difficult to bear at the best of times, but it was combined with such incessant questioning about his future that his nerves were frayed. His state of mind was evident in his reflection – unthinkable at any point over the previous few years – that while in Australia he 'didn't care' if he ever played again.

Perry knew that a top sportsman was only as good as his last match; his likely price for turning professional had diminished as a result of defeat at Forest Hills and withdrawal from the Australian Championships. He also knew he was not sufficiently fit to put up a good showing in any pro tour against the likes of Bill Tilden and Elly Vines. Even so, several American friends advised Perry that he would be 'crazy' not to turn professional soon, having achieved so much in the amateur game. During the course of 1935 the balance of the argument in his mind appears to have shifted firmly, perhaps definitively, in the direction of switching codes.

There was, it seems, only one further possibility that might keep him in the amateur ranks. As Helen was due to be in Britain making a film, he decided to head back earlier than planned to his homeland, hoping that at the 11th hour 'the LTA would turn up with something'.[9]

10

Swapping 'glory for gold'

ARRIVING in England early in 1936 to meet up with his wife, already in the country filming and on the lookout for a London flat, Perry was out of condition and unable to pick up a racket for several more weeks. He was also doubtful that any serious efforts would be made to prevent him from turning professional. His father entered into some behind-the-scenes discussions with Sir Samuel Hoare, the president of the LTA, but these never looked likely to succeed.

The British governing body had not hitherto been confronted with the prospect of a top player threatening to break ranks, and its position remained straightforward: Perry had been amply supported on his various foreign trips and he should abide by the rulebook and be grateful for the chance to represent his nation. Fred claims in his memoirs that Hoare once remarked casually to his father, when discussing the world number one's playing future, 'After all, we do not consider your son to be "one of us".'[1]

It was this attitude that finally pushed Perry over the cliff edge in the autumn of 1936; in describing Fred as not 'one of us', the LTA president was using the same short-hand employed when Brame Hillyard reputedly spoke of the 'best man' not winning the 1934 Wimbledon final.

Sir Samuel Hoare, Conservative MP for Chelsea, was imbued with the ethos characteristic of the upper-middle classes who administered the British game, regarding sport as a pleasant pastime but not a means of gainful employment. Even though out of office at the start of 1936, having resigned as foreign secretary in the National government over the controversial 'Hoare-Laval Pact', the financial concerns of an amateur tennis player rated low on Sir Samuel's list of priorities. In due course he was to become home secretary and a close adviser to Neville Chamberlain in devising the strategy of appeasement towards the fascist dictators.

In his student days Hoare had played tennis to a good standard, although his sport of preference was shooting, at which he excelled and which he described at length in his later works of reminiscence ('Woodcock need a chapter to themselves,' he wrote in one such work). By contrast, Sir Samuel's duties at the LTA after 1932 rated barely a mention when he came to look back on his life of public service.[2]

Hoare's spell out of government in early 1936 proved brief, and as Perry's agitation grew ever stronger the LTA president was concentrating on the demands of a new ministerial role, that of first lord of the Admiralty. For Fred, the only comfort in the short term was a gradual recovery in fitness. With expert medical assistance and renewed training at Highbury with Arsenal's footballers, he returned to the courts in time to defeat Bunny Austin at the British Hard Court Championships in April 1936. From their many encounters Perry knew that Austin's smooth pattern of play could be disrupted by routine acts of gamesmanship, such as hurrying his opponent at times and then taking longer than usual to serve at others. He had plenty to be upset about that day, as Fred swept to a fifth title at Bournemouth, a record that was never to be bettered.

Perry appeared to be returning fully to his best in the French Championships, and exuded his usual assurance as he went out to face Gottfried von Cramm in their third major final within a year. Although the slow surface at Roland Garros made it more difficult for him than it was on grass to hustle his opponent, Perry always felt he had the edge against the German. His victories in the past had been built on using his supreme speed to be in the right place at the right time; von Cramm's exaggerated backswing meant it was possible to read the direction of the ball fairly easily.

But unlike their previous two encounters, the denouement in Paris was played to a different script. As the initiative swung to and fro, each man winning two sets by comfortable margins, Perry looked increasingly flustered. Von Cramm stormed through the final set to love, with the Englishman managing only nine points. The score in the deciding set, it was noted in *The Times*, 'tells its tale of the complete breakdown of Perry, normally the finest fighter of them all for the full distance'.[3]

This was to be Perry's only major defeat in 1936, but it was a dispiriting one. It was a long time since he had been beaten so easily in a fifth-set decider, and he agonised for days afterwards about what caused his abject collapse. He reflected that he was 'mentally flat' after an enforced absence of seven months, and that despite some good performances in Paris, he was still not match-hardened. For the moment the usual Perry exuberance was shattered, and his father wrote him a long letter urging him to pull himself together in the few remaining weeks before Wimbledon.

The warning was timely as the defeat at Roland Garros also had a bearing on the rumbling issue of Perry's playing status. As the silence from the LTA grew more deafening, Fred suspected he was receiving the 'treatment', with the 'bigwigs' in the tennis establishment half-hoping that he would fail to repeat his Wimbledon success, so diminishing his appeal to professional promoters. It was at this moment, Perry reflected, that he resolved, 'come hell or high water', to win once more in SW19 and then to join the pro ranks.[4]

Finally it seems, in the summer of 1936, Perry had decided to step over the precipice: he would leave amateur tennis. But would he go out on a high? He knew that if Wimbledon was lost along with all his other titles, it would look as if he was turning pro because his reputation was on the slide and he was no longer considered a potent threat at the world's top tournaments. The financial offers he might receive to join any professional tour would also almost certainly be less attractive than if he was a three-time Wimbledon champion.

As it was, he progressed steadily, encountering his stiffest opposition in a tough semi-final against Don Budge. The champion had to call on all his resources and experience to change the pattern of the game as it progressed. Instead of attacking the net as he did at the outset, Perry concentrated on moving his opponent around and not letting him get too settled to hit his stinging backhand. After the match, Perry paid an unusually generous public tribute to his opponent.

His claim that the young Californian would inevitably join the roll of champions at Wimbledon soon was both a coded hint that he would not be in the amateur ranks to prevent him from doing so and a background factor in reinforcing his decision to turn professional. He would be making the switch, in the words of Duncan Macaulay, with Donald Budge 'treading very hard on his tail'.[5]

In view of his strained relationship with the British tennis community, it was perhaps fitting that Perry's last appearance in a Wimbledon singles final, against von Cramm, was another anticlimax. The match was shorter and even more one-sided than the 1934 victory over Jack Crawford. After an opening service game by Perry lasting nearly eight minutes, with ten deuces and three break points to von Cramm (each saved by an ace), the final effectively ended as a spectacle when in his first service game the German pulled a muscle in his right leg. By the second set he was limping badly, though he refused either to stop for treatment or to retire, and in just 40 minutes Fred claimed an emphatic 6-1, 6-1, 6-0 success; a score that equalled the previous most one-sided final in Wimbledon history. At the end the umpire spoke to the crowd, once more subdued as Perry took the crown, to relay the baron's apologies that he was unable to make more of a fist of the match owing to injury.[6]

Aside from wanting to avenge defeat in the French Championships, Perry's lack of mercy at Wimbledon indicated that the issue of turning professional was uppermost in his mind. He was anxious that nothing should prevent the process going as smoothly as possible. The die now appeared to be cast. Negotiations were soon to begin between Perry's lawyers and the wealthy entrepreneur (and former Davis Cup player) Frank Hunter and his assistant Howard Voshell, who were in the process of putting together a pro tour in North America for the winter ahead. The sums of money mentioned were more generous than anything previously in the pipeline.

Ted Tinling, present at the Wimbledon Ball after Perry's latest success, observed that alongside many warm tributes for the home player's unprecedented achievements – including a further victory in the mixed doubles with Dorothy Round – some speakers from the top table regretted what was described as the champion's apparent intention to 'desert' the British Davis Cup team. In a forthright response, Perry said he would be glad to continue representing the national team if anyone made it 'worth my while' to do so.[7]

Convinced that the powers-that-be were not genuine about wanting to retain his services, Perry prepared for a swansong on home territory, the defence of the Davis Cup. In contrast to the ease with which the Americans were beaten the previous year, the 1936 Challenge Round against Australia in late July proved a stern test for the British team. On the first day all seemed well as both Perry and Bunny Austin claimed wins against Adrian Quist and Jack Crawford, and although the doubles was lost, English expertise on the Wimbledon grass was expected to prove decisive on the final day. But Austin suffered a rare Davis Cup defeat, against Quist, making the tie all square.

Once again everything rested with Perry in the deciding rubber, this time against Crawford. Dan Maskell, on hand throughout as the assiduous team coach, recalled, 'Fred did not fail us.' Playing with 'exemplary coolness' on a rain-interrupted day, he attacked remorselessly and came through 6-2, 6-2, 6-3 in about an hour. 'It was a glorious moment. Britain was truly top of the world,' wrote Maskell, having emulated the British team of the Dohertys that won the cup four successive times from 1903 to 1906.[8]

It was doubtful that Perry at this point shared Maskell's sense of excitement. As was the case for much of the summer of 1936, his mind was on other things. While he admitted to a 'great love affair' with Wimbledon as a venue and a tournament, Perry had reached a parting of the ways with the people who held sway at the AEC and the LTA, exclaiming, 'Nothing had been done to encourage me to stay in the amateur game.'

At the 11th hour, there were attempts on his behalf among businessmen led by Albert Slazenger to coordinate a scheme that might provide him with a legitimate income, but those contacted mostly felt Perry should be proud to represent his country without financial reward. No announcements about turning pro were forthcoming over the summer, but as Fred travelled to New York it was an open secret that he was on the verge of leaving the amateur game. His main reason for holding back from putting pen to paper on a contract was that he decided he wanted to go out in style; he hoped to repeat his Wimbledon success with a third triumph in the American Championships.

He had also set his heart on ending his days as an amateur at one of his favourite tournaments, the Pacific Southwest in California. In the event the plan was to be carried out to perfection – almost.

At Forest Hills in September he beat six Americans on his way to the final, dropping only two sets. He then faced Budge, the American who provided the stiffest resistance at Wimbledon back in the summer. On what the renowned tennis journalist Wallis Myers called a 'steamy, enervating afternoon', a 12,000-strong crowd witnessed 'one of the most strenuous and exciting struggles' ever contested at Forest Hills as the protagonists battled it out for nearly three hours.[9]

After a see-saw struggle, the fifth and final set was one of the most dramatic passages of play in Perry's career. The expectation was that his famed fitness would enable him to pull clear in the decider, though it was Budge who took the initiative, and who had every chance when he served at 5-3 for the title. But nerves got the better of the American as he opened with a double fault and then lost his service following several tentative shots. Perry held and eventually, serving at 9-8, indulged in some arch gamesmanship on match point. Having kept a spare ball in his pocket throughout the game, he pulled it out unexpectedly and sent down a rapid ace before Budge could properly set himself. He never ascertained whether his opponent was ready or not, but he dashed to the net to shake hands and the deed was done.

It was an unsurpassable climax to Perry's amateur career. As the first three-time overseas winner of the American Championships, he took permanent possession of the trophy. Fittingly, it was his unrivalled fitness, fighting quality and guile that carried him over the line one last time. There was, however, a price to be paid.

His love of California explained his desire to make one more appearance at the Pacific Southwest, but it proved difficult for Perry after travelling west to summon the same physical and mental energies for a rematch with Budge, especially as the higher bounce on the cement courts in Los Angeles favoured his opponent. Perry admitted, with the lawyers finalising the terms of his professional contract, that he wasn't any longer in the right frame of mind. This final part of his exit strategy was thus a let-down. Jack Kramer later reflected that for him as an aspiring 15-year-old watching in the stands it 'really hurt' to see a star player 'quit', which he claims Perry did, adding that Fred never seemed troubled by defeat.[10]

While this may have been accurate as far as the Pacific Southwest Final was concerned, it was an unfair verdict more broadly on Perry, whose hatred of losing had been vital in propelling and sustaining him at the top of the game. Kramer overlooked the fact that Vines (whom Kramer admired as the best player of the period) put in many below-par performances when unsettled in the months before he turned professional. Perry might also have retorted that although he lost twice to Budge in 1936 (in a USA–Britain friendly at Eastbourne on the eve of the Davis Cup Challenge Round, as well as in Los Angeles), he prevailed in their two most important encounters: at Wimbledon and Forest Hills.

Defeat in the Pacific Southwest was in any event soon forgotten when confirmation of Perry's switch to professional tennis was finally announced at the Wall Street offices of his lawyer in New York on 6 November. The initial agreement was that he would go head-to-head with Elly Vines and others in North America on a five-month tour starting in January 1937, with a figure of $100,000 mentioned as his minimum income from a guaranteed proportion of gate receipts.

In the weeks after Perry's departure from amateur tennis was confirmed, strong opinions were offered from sharply contrasting perspectives. Reflecting a concern that the Davis Cup was certain to be lost to Britain, some newspapers accused Perry of having swapped 'glory for gold', a term first coined by the *Philadelphia Inquirer*. Others however, such as the left-leaning *Manchester Guardian*, felt that 'no fair-minded person will upbraid him'; a sentiment echoed from within the tennis community by Davis Cup coach Dan Maskell, who reflected that the time had come for Fred to 'capitalise on all the hard work and dedication that had made him the greatest champion of his generation'.[11]

But from the game's governing body in Britain, the response was stern and unforgiving. Perry was told that, notwithstanding his status as world number one, he would be relieved forthwith of his honorary membership of the All England Club (bestowed as Wimbledon champion) and barred from membership of LTA-affiliated clubs. Although some generous references to Perry were made at the LTA's annual general meeting in December 1936, at the same time the governing body's official journal referred disparagingly to him having decided to 'seek his fortune in the ranks of the exhibition player'.[12]

In terms of where responsibility lay for this sour outcome, it seems fair to conclude that the blame did not all rest on one side. Reflecting on the whole sorry episode years later, Perry admitted to being inflexible and 'uncompromising' at times. He also acknowledged that with his focus on playing and winning, he 'never took the time to understand' those who ran the LTA.

In the calmer perspective of later life, he also tried to see the issue from the authorities' point of view. Perry recognised that some of what he faced was a defensive reaction to the threat of losing a key Davis Cup performer, especially in circumstances that had not arisen in Britain before.[13] These admissions underline the point that the LTA should at least be credited with trying to preserve Britain's place in world tennis. The governing body, after all, had chosen Perry to represent Britain as early as 1930 and regularly funded his overseas trips thereafter.

One of his fellow British players, Ted Avory, felt that Perry's mistake was to regard the tennis establishment as monolithic and uniformly hostile, rather than being a collection of separate entities and characters of varying sympathies. 'I had no title and no land and there were clubs I simply never tried to join,' Avory tried telling Perry. 'But Fred never really saw that.'[14]

In view of the dialogue of the deaf that took place between Perry and the LTA in the mid-1930s, a parting of the ways was probably unavoidable. But could and should the governing body have done more to retain its star player? While conceding he was not blameless, it still rankled with Perry when he wrote his memoirs, 50 years on from the heat of battle, that the LTA refused to engage in discussion about possible ways forward, hiding instead he felt behind traditions and regulations. He disliked intensely the claim that nothing could be done because of the amateur rulebook, believing that a solution could have been worked out if there was a genuine will.[15]

Perry was alluding here to the double standards whereby some governing bodies elsewhere in the world in the 1930s, while espousing the virtues of amateurism in theory, were in practice turning a blind eye to breaches of the rules in order to maintain strong Davis Cup squads. France had been known to make efforts to retain its musketeers who delivered Davis Cup success for several years and in Australia, it was becoming common for sporting goods companies to employ or subsidise the best players, so enabling them to develop full-time amateur careers. But in Britain, he felt, no subtle financial arrangements of the type others benefited from were on the table. Instead, as noted earlier, the LTA flatly refused after 1934 to even accept that amateurs should be entitled to eight weeks of legitimate expenses per year.

In view of its long-standing and hard-line commitment to amateur principles, it was hardly surprising that the LTA refused to regard Perry as a special case. Indeed the LTA took comfort from the knowledge that – despite Perry joining Vines and others in successful money-making tours after 1936 – the amateur authorities remained firmly in the ascendant through to the Second World War and beyond. In contrast to the lavish media coverage of major amateur tournaments, pro tours barely rated a mention on the sports pages or the radio airwaves. The enduring popularity and success of top amateur events meant that governing bodies worldwide, including the LTA, were able to treat pro tennis largely as an irrelevance.

Although the signing of ex-Wimbledon champions such as Perry made for greater credibility, professional promoters knew their 'product' would become stale if it could only promise endless match-ups between a tiny band of players. Amateur administrators, confident that the established game would always throw up new stars bursting to make a breakthrough, even believed that pro tours – starved of a string of high-quality recruits – might fizzle out and disappear altogether.[16]

In the final analysis, perhaps the most damning charge against the LTA was that it made so little effort to part with Perry on anything like reasonable terms. In 1938 Don Budge – after becoming the first player to win all four grand slam titles in a calendar year – was given a warm send-off by the US Tennis Association when he turned pro, despite the American tennis establishment, like the British, being renowned for its dim view of 'defectors'.[17]

American administrators, perhaps heeding the lesson of how the LTA handled its own renegade, felt it was right to show gratitude to Budge, who in Perry's absence helped the USA to beat Britain and reclaim the Davis Cup in 1937 for the first time in more than a decade. By contrast, Perry was to be something of a tennis outcast in his homeland for many years to come. After all he had achieved individually and as part of Britain's Davis Cup team (winning 34 of 38 singles rubbers and 11 of 14 doubles contests in that competition), Perry was left with an immense and lasting sense of rejection.

Fifty years later, in his autobiography, his enduring sense of grievance at being treated in such a way still came through loud and clear, 'I always had the feeling that I was tolerated but not really wanted.'[18]

It was time to move on.

11

Life on the pro tour

A N EXCITING, sometimes tumultuous, new chapter in Perry's life opened up in 1937. The tour organised by Frank Hunter's business group began amid great fanfare at Madison Square Garden in New York on the night of 6 January. In front of a packed auditorium with in excess of 17,000 spectators, a bright spotlight fell on Perry as he entered, and a public address system announced in booming tones, 'Presenting the world's amateur champion, Frederick J. Perry.'

The audience stood to the sound of 'God Save the King' before the spotlight shifted across the arena to fix on 'Ellsworth Vines, the professional champion of the world,' whose arrival was accompanied by the playing of 'The Star-Spangled Banner'. The extravagant big build-up – unknown in the serene surroundings of Wimbledon

– set the scene for the first of many encounters over the coming years between the two erstwhile amateur champions and rivals, men of very different playing styles and temperaments.

This was the world of professional tennis, and the English challenger – relieved after the anguish that preceded his decision to turn pro to be back on court doing what he did best – appeared to relish every moment. According to the doubles specialist George Lott, who made up part of the touring group, Perry on that evening was in his element, enjoying the razzmatazz and delighted to confound the New York press by beating Vines in a three-set match. In the view of Lott, 'All in all, one Frederick J. Perry was having the time of his life.' The Englishman immodestly said afterwards in conversation, 'Don't you think I played as good tennis as was ever played?'

His sense of satisfaction was enhanced by knowing this was the first of what would be several lucrative pay-days. Gate receipts almost reached a massive $60,000, of which Perry pocketed close to $13,000 and Vines around $5,000. The division of the spoils was based not on the outcome of the match but the convention on such tours that the incoming professional received the lion's share at the outset. It was the novelty of pitting the world's top ex-amateur against established pros that drew in the crowds, and the promoters ended the evening persuaded that Perry had been worth every dollar.[1]

Lott smiled wryly to himself as he watched the Perry–Vines encounter, aware from experience that the long tour ahead would be different when it 'hit the sticks' outside New York. Perry discovered soon enough that the relatively leisurely pace of week- or two-week-long amateur tournaments was a thing of the past. 'Barnstorming professional tennis tours can only be likened to one-night vaudeville stands,' wrote Lott.

The 'Britisher', as the promoters liked to call him, was pitched into a fast and furious way of life, travelling by train or car up to 500 miles at night between venues after finishing an evening schedule of singles and doubles. Before long Perry had played on successive nights in New York, Chicago, Milwaukee and Pittsburgh. He also had to get used to a bewildering variety of indoor venues, playing in anything from local gyms to ice rinks. Wherever the tour went a canvas court – transported round via truck and stretched with pulleys – was laid flush on top of the existing surface. Outdoor playing conditions could be particularly challenging. On a sticky and humid night in Omaha, the players had to contend not only with temperatures of about 90 degrees Fahrenheit, but also with the attention of black beetles buzzing around incessantly. Fred recollected that whenever he jumped up for a smash he would 'squash a couple very noisily' as he landed.'[2]

The tour suffered an early setback when Vines, who contracted flu in New York, was admitted to hospital with nervous exhaustion. Fortunately Bill Tilden was on hand to deputise. Although now in his 40s, Tilden was still remarkably fit, and Perry only narrowly edged ahead 4-3 in a hastily improvised mini-series. When Vines returned he played with much of his old verve, and at the end of the American leg of the tour he held a 32-29 lead over Perry. Living and working in close proximity inevitably produced tensions between the laid-back Vines and the ebullient crowd-pleaser Perry. But for the most part bust-ups were rare and soon forgotten as the road show moved on. Despite the various difficulties, the early months of the 1937 tour were considered a major success, attracting large crowds everywhere it went. As Perry realised, part of the reason so many locals turned up was that they hoped to see the 'Britisher' take a beating.

If, however, Perry the professional hoped his differences with the amateur authorities in Britain would quickly be forgiven and forgotten, and that he would be welcomed with open arms in his homeland, he was disabused when the tour travelled to Europe later in the spring of 1937.

Plans to play in England were almost aborted when all clubs affiliated to the LTA were barred from staging Perry–Vines matches. It was only through the intervention of one of Fred's old school friends, businessman Bernard Sunley, that a portable wooden tennis court was constructed and transported around to outdoor venues at football clubs in cities such as Bristol and Liverpool.

Perry won narrowly in a seven-match outdoor series, and there was a similar outcome in the King George VI Coronation Cup, held over three nights at Wembley's Empire Pool in May. Crowds were reasonable at most British venues, with 9,000 paying customers each night at Wembley (and 10,000 on the Kop at Anfield), though the strongest impression of this leg of the tour was the wrath of British officialdom.

In effect it was time for the LTA's payback for what some administrators felt was Perry's desertion of the national team. 'In European tennis, "pro" was still a dirty word,' he later recalled. Far from being a tennis hero, the three-time Wimbledon champion was cold-shouldered in his own backyard. As well as being barred from appearing on the courts of affiliated clubs, he was asked to tender his resignation from those clubs of which he was a member, in addition to the All England Club, on the grounds that membership was open only to amateurs. Even though this was done reluctantly by some of the clubs Fred played at in his early years, and despite the public appetite for watching the professionals at work, it was clear there would be no LTA campaign in the late 1930s to find and cultivate new champions in the wake of Perry's achievements.

In 1938 the governing body was still fighting a rearguard action against widening the level of legitimate expenses available to amateurs, its stance prompting accusations of a head in the sand mentality from hitherto loyal players such as Ted Avory and Harold Lee. In the meantime, as the unreformed and unrepentant LTA went its own way, by far the most successful player the nation had produced since the First World War became almost a non-person in the eyes of the authorities, airbrushed out of tennis history.[3]

Although the level of hostility that greeted him in some quarters in Britain took him aback, on the whole Perry was more than satisfied with his first experience of professional tennis. When the tour ended with some final matches back in the United States, Vines retained the unofficial title of World Professional Champion. But 'the Britisher' had earned considerably more money. Gross receipts came to some $400,000.

As with all such tours, both before and later, the players did have to contend with accusations that they were only playing exhibition tennis. Some newspapers alleged that results were pre-arranged to keep audiences interested, and according to Vines's adopted son, his father was asked by the promoters – fearful that attendances would drop as they had when Vines got well ahead of Tilden in earlier series – to keep things close if there was a danger of him winning too easily, a suggestion with which he reluctantly agreed.[4]

Not surprisingly, the players took a different view. Perry was insistent that though he was to vie with Vines on some 350 occasions in pro matches, there was no match-fixing of any sort; rather both players always put in maximum effort to come out on top. On one occasion, he admits that – with an early start required the following day for a long journey to the next venue – the two men agreed that whoever prevailed in the first set of their evening match should be given an easier time in the second set to hasten proceedings. But in the event hard-wired competitive instincts took over and a tense, lengthy three-setter ensued.[5]

Vines made no reference to collusion in his frequent letters home to his wife (which usually contained great detail about his thoughts) and George Lott also maintained that fixing never took place, pointing to the 'no quarter given' spirit in which the Perry–Vines matches were conducted. Lott concurred with Perry's view: despite each pulling out all the stops on court, the two main protagonists, apart from the occasional spat, enjoyed each other's company on tour and gradually developed a real bond.[6]

Perry's relationship with Vines prompted him to embark on the first of many business ventures in his post-amateur life. Using their earnings from the 1937 tour, the two friends bought a stake in the Beverly Hills Tennis Club, a six-court complex set in the hills above Los Angeles. The club had been set up to ensure the privacy of its hundred or so members: mostly actors, directors, writers and studio heads. The new owners held a grand re-launch opening, featuring another Anglo-American contest of less seriousness than on the professional tour;

a doubles contest between Perry, partnered with Charlie Chaplin, and Vines playing with Groucho Marx.

The ethos remained that of providing an opportunity for movie people to get away from the hurly-burly of Hollywood. At the club, Perry said, the stars 'could let their hair down, so a lot of crazy things went on', many of them associated with one of Hollywood's most riotous characters, Errol Flynn.[7]

Vines's adopted son claims his father, much less attached to the Hollywood lifestyle than his business partner, was uncomfortable with the 'constant notoriety', though Vines himself later spoke proudly of the project, which he said worked well apart from the need to leave others in charge during the frequent absence of the co-owners. It was through his day-to-day contact with many of the best-known movie stars of the day, including the likes of Marlene Dietrich, Douglas Fairbanks, David Niven and Bebe Daniels, that Perry fulfilled a further ambition denied him in his amateur days, playing a small cameo role as a tennis player in a 1937 MGM film. According to the well-known tennis writer Richard Evans, Perry was the toast of Hollywood, 'Where the wrong accent did not matter. Most of them were manufactured anyway.'[8]

In the short term, Perry had no regrets about his decision to quit amateur tennis. He found the United States a congenial and welcoming home, and he was soon making formal moves to secure US citizenship. His treatment in his native land on his trip in 1937 confirmed in his own mind that he had done the right thing, and he was not inclined to be hard on himself when Britain lost its hold on the Davis Cup later in the year. Britain's brief era of domination in world tennis during the mid-1930s, with success in both the men's and women's game, came to a shuddering halt. The Davis Cup team without Perry was, as Dan Maskell remarked, 'like *Hamlet* without the Prince'.[9]

In the Challenge Round held at Wimbledon in July, the British were no match for a strong United States team spearheaded by Donald Budge, indisputably the new king of the amateur scene. Still aged only 21, Budge went through most of the 1937 season undefeated, his supremacy built on overwhelming power combined with superb concentration and mental strength.

Perry was no longer part of the set-up dominated by Budge, but he had the comfort of remaining an attraction in the USA, as was evident when large crowds were attracted to the initial contests of his second tour with Vines in the early months of 1938. This broke fresh ground by moving away from the usual venues in the north-east of the country. Instead new audiences were sought out in several southern states, a decision made partly to allow Vines to combine tennis with his new passion, golf.

By entering circuit tournaments, Vines took the first steps towards becoming a fully fledged (and highly successful) golf professional. Some of Vines's interest also rubbed off on Fred, who became a more than proficient golfer, prefiguring his later move into golf management as a business proposition. On court the pattern of the previous year was repeated with Perry winning the first six matches in a row but Vines pulling back to take the lead (49-35) by the time the tour ended in May.

Fred therefore enjoyed a honeymoon phase in his new life across the Atlantic, giving himself a measure of financial independence that he had never previously known and at the same time mixing with the great and the good of Hollywood at his Beverley Hills club. But not everything was rosy in the garden. Despite the pulling power of the early encounters, and in spite of putting on more matches in total, receipts from the 1938 tour were significantly smaller – by about two-thirds – than in 1937.

The fall in revenue resulted in part from there being no European leg to the pro tour in 1938. This had less to do with Perry being unwelcome on British shores and more to do with fiscal concerns: his wife, Helen Vinson, had made big-earning movies in England for the previous two years but paid no tax. If he went to London, he would run the risk of the Inland Revenue demanding that he settle Helen's tax bill, something he would find difficult given that his marriage was on the rocks.

In a frank assessment in his memoirs, Perry blamed his marital problems on long absences, and admitted that bitterness set in as lengthy legal proceedings to finalise a divorce dragged on. Perry claimed Helen's lawyers made his life difficult, insisting for example that locks on the doors be changed, leaving him temporarily with just the clothes he was wearing. The divorce settlement, when it came, adversely affected Fred's finances for several years to come.

After two seasons with Perry and Vines being in the spotlight, public enthusiasm for pro tennis in the United States was also waning. It was vital if momentum was to be regained that new blood be recruited. It was a major relief and boon for the pros when it was announced they would be joined by Donald Budge, who in 1938 became the first man to win all four grand slam events in the same calendar year.

Embroiled in the fall-out from his marital break-up, Perry found it difficult to apply himself fully when the 1939 professional tour got under way. In his amateur days he got the better of Budge in head-to-head encounters. But circumstances had changed considerably since the last meeting of the two men in 1936. Whereas Budge was unbeatable after that and in his physical prime, Perry was approaching his 30th birthday, and suffered from no longer being exposed to the variety and depth of competition found in the amateur game. He also felt the fast indoor courts used in the pro tours favoured his hard-hitting American opponents, giving him little opportunity to mix up the play and use his renowned court-craft in long rallies.

In the traditional tour opener staged at Madison Square Garden in March 1939, Budge blasted Perry for the loss of only four games in three sets; the whole thing was over in 49 minutes. While determined at the time to give no quarter, the American later agreed that 'the rout removed a lot of the drama from the tour from the first'.[10]

Perry managed to win only one set in their first seven matches, and although he improved steadily, Budge was still comfortably ahead – by 28 victories to eight – when the tour came to an end, as he was in his separate contests against Vines. The Vines–Budge series was held first, in the early weeks of 1939, an indication that Perry had been ousted as the headline attraction on the pro circuit.

The recognition that many of the matches were one-sided made it difficult to attract large crowds. Only 7,000 spectators watched Perry's New York opener in March, and the gross receipts of all the tour matches in 1939, at just over $250,000, was well short of what was achieved in 1937. Rounding off a period of unhappiness, Perry also lost the US Pro title in 1939. He secured this the previous year but, with Budge not participating, Perry was beaten by Vines in a final held at the Beverly Hills club. Although the match contained some of their finest ever exchanges, especially in a 20-18 fourth set that sealed victory for Vines, relinquishing the title was hard to take.

When war in Europe broke out in September 1939 Perry found himself, according to his memoirs, 'terribly torn'. Should he return to join the fight against Nazi

Germany or should he stay in his recently adopted homeland? Detractors in Britain hinted that Perry was shown in his true light (as a so-called 'bomb dodger') by opting not to fight for his country, though as we have seen he had harboured thoughts about making the United States his home for several years, going back to long before the outbreak of war. His thinking was perhaps ultimately swayed by the prospect that if he returned he would have to abandon the new life he had chosen and start all over again.

He decided to stay where he was, with the proviso that he would 'go into the American services if and when they got into the war', although in practice he was called up by the US authorities rather than volunteering.[11] Among other things, this allowed him to continue for a while playing some high standard tennis; an option not available in Europe, where the amateur game came to a shuddering halt.

Pro tennis in the United States was at least able to stumble along in the early war years, with some of its proceeds being directed towards supporting the Allied cause. In 1941 Budge was absent from most challenge matches and Perry was able to dominate against lesser-known players, taking the US Pro title for the second time by winning in Chicago. Yet with hindsight Perry had to admit that in 1940/41 his heart and his priorities were not in tennis. He was still resentful about the divorce from Helen and he wanted to be left to his own devices.

In the winter months especially, he avoided too much unwelcome company by spending long periods in Mexico, where he built some contacts after playing exhibition matches with Vines. Perry was asked to take over the tennis set up at a country club just outside Mexico City, an offer that allowed him to lodge in a cottage on the site whenever he came to stay.

An unsettled spell in Perry's life continued to take some dramatic twists and turns as the conflict in Europe intensified. In 1941 he met and wed a glamorous American fashion model, Sandra Breaux. Despite the romantic setting of a wedding in Mexico, this second marriage – like his first – was soon to end in divorce.

Fred also experienced a life-changing moment on court. After the American national championships at Forest Hills in 1941 both of the finalists, Bobby Riggs and Frank Kovacs, signed with the promoter Lex Thompson, owner of the Philadelphia Eagles. The plan was to stimulate fresh interest in professional tennis by pitting the up-and-coming pretenders against the established pros Budge and Perry, who were offered $25,000 as a minimum for their involvement.

But the timing of the proposed tour could not have been worse. The Japanese attack on Pearl Harbor on 7 December focused the nation's full attention on entering the war but, after much agonising, it was decided to go ahead as planned, though the public had little appetite for watching tennis.

176

In the opening matches at Madison Square Garden, just a few weeks after Pearl Harbor, Riggs was leading 5-4 against Perry in the final set when the Englishman fell awkwardly, failing to notice a tear in the synthetic surface. He was catapulted up in the air and severely damaged his right elbow. Perry's injury was a serious blow for the tour, which struggled into 1942 but was cancelled a month earlier than scheduled.[12]

It was also a major personal setback for Fred. From hospital he travelled to Mexico to recuperate, painfully aware that the almost unthinkable had happened: his days of front-line competitive tennis were over.

12

Coach, commentator, businessman

THE years of America's involvement in the Second World War were not the best of times for Perry. The demands of military life; the need to contemplate a future that did not involve playing high-level pro tennis; ongoing marital problems – all required Fred, now in his 30s, to re-evaluate his priorities and ponder what should come next. In the short term the dictates of war were paramount.

After Pearl Harbor, Perry was conscripted and passed fit for military service. For propaganda purposes, US military leaders regarded it as important that top athletes were seen in uniform, entertaining fellow troops if not actually going to the front line. Donald Budge spent much of his time after 1941 playing exhibition matches for servicemen in the Pacific Islands, while Fred became a physical trainer and rehabilitation officer based in California.

Perry's role certainly made for a less harrowing wartime experience than some of those he locked horns with in his amateur days. Gottfried von Cramm, who resisted attempts to coerce him into joining the Nazi party, was sent to the Russian front and eventually received the Iron Cross for bravery. Bunny Austin, like Perry, faced accusations of lacking patriotism by continuing to work in the USA, as he had for several years, for the religious body Moral Rearmament (an action that resulted in the cancellation of Austin's AEC membership, not to be renewed until 1984). Perry did though believe that working with wounded servicemen made a useful contribution to the American cause. Following the final surrender of Japan, he was eventually discharged from his role as staff sergeant in the autumn of 1945.[1]

At the end of the year, Perry was about to leave to spend some time in Mexico when Bill Tilden arrived at the Beverly Hills club and persuaded him to play some exhibition tennis for soldiers unable to get home for Christmas. Perry was reluctant, saying he had lost 'interest and confidence', and knowing his injury would prevent him from hitting the ball with any force. He took no part in the small amount of pro tennis that continued in America after the ill-fated tour of 1941/42, and when a newly formed World Professional Tennis Association issued a list of top ten performers late in 1945 Perry's name did not appear. Although his arm shook and was painful, picking up a racket did provide a way back into the game, especially as there was the buzz of appearing again in front of film stars and celebrities, anxious to see good quality tennis resumed.

Perry subsequently agreed to take part in an eight-month tournament schedule across the United States during 1946 organised by Tilden. This was a new departure for pro tennis. In contrast to the pre-war model of nightly city-by-city appearances featuring the same tiny group of players, the 1946 circuit was closer to the amateur game in bringing larger numbers together to compete for a week at a time. With few new star recruits because of wartime disruption, Perry was strong enough to be ranked fourth – after Riggs, Budge and Kovacs – at the end of the circuit, though he claimed in his memoirs that he mainly filled in when his arm was not too sore. He was unable to hit with any great pace, particularly with his backhand cross court, and had to 'fiddle his shots', he said.[2]

As a result of advancing age and injury, Perry was in effect easing back from the supreme level of play he sustained prior to 1942. For someone with fierce competitive instincts it was little consolation at this point in his life (unlike later, when he looked back with great pride on his achievements), that his name was in the records books and resonated around the world. As the amateur circuit resumed, it was noticeable that many of the top players were compared with Perry in his prime. The winner of the first post-war Wimbledon in 1946, Frenchman Yvon Petra, modelled his aggressive style partly on Perry's, mixing a hard service with a lethal forehand, not to mention what the tennis journalist Norman Cutler called an 'inability to win gracefully'.[3]

In 1948 the Wimbledon crowds reacted angrily when the Californian Bob Falkenburg employed controversial stalling tactics, taking long breaks between points, and at times throwing himself on the ground. Under questioning from journalists, Falkenburg – who went onto take the title – commented that it was Fred Perry who had told him not to hurry on court; he was merely taking advice from one of the great tacticians of the game.

In later years the American insisted he did nothing against the rules and that it was up to the umpire, not the crowd and the press, to hold him to account if necessary. Although it was later revealed that Falkenburg was suffering from a rare medical condition resulting in sluggishness, his behaviour was greeted in 1948 as a sign that post-war amateur tennis was being taken with greater than ever seriousness. Perry had clearly played a part in this.

Professional tennis after 1945 was also moving on and becoming more business-oriented. Amateur authorities around the world hitherto regarded the pro game as an irritant more than a genuine threat, believing it might fade away for lack of a constant stream of quality recruits. Bill Tilden's 1946 circuit was a shot across the bows, 'pioneering stuff' Perry called it, a precursor to the later era in which tennis players were openly paid to perform all year round.

But in 1947 Tilden was jailed for indecency offences, and his tour concept collapsed overnight. It was vital to the continuance and revival of pro tennis that the experienced promoter Jack Harris was able to recruit Jack Kramer, the leading amateur of the day, for a head-to-head tour in 1948 with Bobby Riggs. Kramer's arrival marked a major long-term threat to the amateur game, of which he was relentlessly critical; in the 1950s he was to become the chief organiser of numerous professional tours.

Pro tennis had brought Perry variety, the opportunity for extensive travel, and also wealth. Even allowing for the costs of divorce and lost earnings through injury, his friend and later business rival Ted Tinling believed Fred earned close to a million dollars in the decade after he left the amateur game in 1936 for what was termed 'huge money for that era'.[4]

It had not, however, produced contentment on the domestic front. After parting from his second wife, he embarked on a third marriage in 1945, to Lorraine Walsh – sister of the actor Walter Pidgeon – but before long this ended in the same way as the earlier two, in divorce. The reality was that Perry was at a crossroads. Pro tennis was increasingly dominated by a rising generation that included the likes of Pancho Gonzales and Pancho Segura as well as Jack Kramer, and Perry's appearances on court were becoming so infrequent that from 1950 on he was only infrequently included in listings of top professionals.

The focus of his life was changing. He gradually began to develop a range of new activities that revolved mostly around coaching, commentating and business initiatives. All of these, in differing ways, kept him in the spotlight of tennis, and ensured his name remained well known in his later years, even though the days of being centre stage as one of the world's best players were gone.

One indication of Perry's life moving in fresh directions was his return, after an 11-year absence, to austerity-ravaged Britain in 1947. He may have been an international sporting celebrity, but he was still a long way from being rehabilitated by the tennis authorities in his homeland. He came to Britain not at the instigation of the LTA – which for the time being continued to largely cold-shoulder the former Wimbledon champion – but at the behest of his racket sponsors, Slazenger. Part of his reason for accepting the invitation was the opportunity after a long spell apart to see his father, retired from his job at the Co-op party, and other members of his family. As a US citizen he was permitted to stay in Britain for only a limited number of days per year, and having no base of his own he stayed in Ealing for some of the visit. As he noted in his memoirs, however, perhaps referring to the presence of another child in the house who was the centre of attention following Sam's second marriage, 'things weren't…quite the same'.[5]

In many other respects he did find Britain much as he left it: times were hard for the majority of ordinary people under Attlee's Labour government as the nation sought to recover from six years of war. Another thing that had not changed was that, as in the late 1930s after he left the country to embark on pro tours in America, there was no attempt by the LTA to use his name to inspire a new generation of tennis champions. In emergency wartime conditions amateur tennis was largely suspended for the duration, and unlike in the USA simply reviving the game was a difficult task. Perry teamed up with old friend Dan Maskell to play exhibition matches, donating the proceeds to clubs for repairs and improvements. Maskell told him it was an uphill struggle; no child under ten was likely to have watched or participated in any meaningful tennis.

There were other reasons for coming to Britain in 1947. Perry made his way to London SW19 for the Wimbledon fortnight: the first time he visited an amateur tournament since the Forest Hills Final of 1936. He went not as the guest of the All England Club, but rather as an observer to write daily columns for the *London Evening Standard*. Returning to the scene of some of his greatest triumphs rekindled Perry's love for the venue, and the Wimbledon fortnight became a regular part of his summer routine over the years that followed.

In 1948 he was invited to broadcast on radio alongside Max Robertson of the BBC, and from this time on Perry could count on a steady income as a well-informed, pungent and incisive commentator for newspapers, radio or television, including a brief spell for ITV. His ability to analyse matches and to appreciate the finer points of tactics – a major cause of his own success on court – made him ideally suited to the commentating role, and until near the end of his life he was never to miss a day's play at the Championships.[6]

Starting in 1948, Perry's stay in England was extended further into the summer months by his involvement in a coaching initiative led by Maskell. The LTA after the war swiftly revived local tournament structures, serving the interests of keener players, but Maskell wanted to find ways of extending the popularity of the game to those with no prior experience, and with this in mind he accepted the leadership of a 'Focus on Tennis' project.

This was the brainchild of the Central Council of Physical Recreation (CCPR), the independent voluntary body committed to boosting participation in sport. The idea was for youngsters to be introduced to tennis in the school holidays through demonstrations and coaching clinics. With Slazenger providing the equipment, Perry accompanied Maskell on a hectic schedule, driving long distances that took them as far as Cornwall in one direction and north-east England in the other. Play was organised on football pitches, in indoor markets, or anywhere an audience could be gathered. Boys and girls were encouraged to hit some balls and would then watch Perry and Maskell play a set of exhibition tennis.

The former Wimbledon champion, immaculately turned out as always, made a lasting impression on some of the youngsters. Alan Mills, later a Wimbledon referee, was a teenager in the late 1940s and confessed to being 'completely star-struck' when he attended one of the clinics. He said, 'I practised with Fred, and I recall being amazed at how hard he hit the ball.'[7]

For Perry it was an enjoyable first foray into the world of tennis coaching. As a CCPR-backed project he was not required to have any direct contact with the LTA, and yet at the same time he could make a contribution to the rebuilding of British tennis. His enjoyment was such that he was happy to repeat the experience for three years running. The most promising youngsters, he recalled, were sent for more intensive coaching with Maskell at the AEC. Out of the scheme emerged Davis Cup players in the 1950s and 1960s such as Billy Knight and Mike Sangster, as well as Angela Buxton, 'so our efforts were not wasted'.[8]

Coaching also became a prominent feature of Perry's life in his adopted homeland. After the everyday shortages and hardships of Britain, he returned to the

US in the autumn of 1947 to find an offer waiting for the position of teaching pro at the luxurious Boca Raton hotel in Palm Beach, Florida. Built at a cost of $18m in the 1920s, the hotel had superb facilities, and Perry decided that, in the aftermath of three failed marriages, he had little to lose by moving right across America from California to Florida – his US base for the rest of his life.

It was one of the best decisions he made, enabling him to spend 13 happy years at this unrivalled location. He bought a house nearby and travelled the half-mile to work via a boat on the inland waterway. From October through to May each year Perry worked as a coach, teaching the sons and daughters of millionaires, mostly drawn from wealthy Jewish-American families. Eventually a change of ownership saw the hotel under threat, though coaching in any case was gradually superseded in Fred's priorities by a new venture. As he wrote in his memoirs, his life rather unexpectedly 'branched out in another direction: the clothing business'.[9]

It was during one of his visits to Britain in the late 1940s that Perry became involved, almost by accident, in a scheme that ensured he remained a wealthy man for the rest of his days. He candidly conceded that from the 1950s onwards his name was best known throughout the world – as it remains today – less for winning Wimbledon three times, 'but because of Fred Perry shirts and sportswear'.

While taking part in the Focus on Tennis scheme with Maskell, he was approached out of the blue by an

Austrian former footballer called Theo (Tibby) Wegner, who wanted to use the tennis player's name to market a sweatband he had designed. Perry told him to go away and adapt what was initially a cumbersome and unattractive product, thinking that would be the end of the story. To his surprise Wegner reappeared a few weeks later having made the sweatband lighter, softer and more pliable. At the time this seemed like a modest, small-scale proposal and Fred felt there was little to lose in offering his support. He suspected from his own experience that there would be a market for a device to stop perspiration running down the arm and making the racket grip slippery. It was with no great ambition in mind that the Fred Perry sportswear company was launched.

The company expanded from its small beginnings by diversifying initially into the production and sale of good-quality white tennis shirts for men. The Fred Perry polo shirt, launched at Wimbledon in 1952, was instantly recognisable from a trademark laurel wreath stitched on the front; an idea based on a pre-war symbol used at Wimbledon. It was a sign of slowly improving relations that written permission was granted by the All England Club for use of the wreath as a logo, although in practice the AEC admitted to owning no rights to the emblem and had ceased using it after 1945.

Wegner took the lead in persuading a company in Leicester to produce 75 dozen shirts using white knitted cotton pique. Perry was tasked with marketing and selling. His reputation gave him access to the dressing rooms at Wimbledon where he could conduct promotional work. He found the new generation of young Australians coming to prominence in amateur tennis, the likes of Lew Hoad and Ken Rosewall, particularly receptive as they hitherto travelled mostly with 'boring old sagging shirts'. Before long the example of Wimbledon champions sporting the shirt generated a wider market among club players, especially in an age of growing television coverage of the Championships. By using contacts in London, Perry was soon receiving large bulk orders for major shops in the capital such as Lillywhites and Harrods, 'Next time we made 400 dozen, and that's how Fred Perry Sportswear hit the jackpot.'[10]

By the end of the 1950s the company was a brand leader in the sportswear field, with regular orders in America alone worth half a million dollars. This position was maintained until the post-1968 open era witnessed an explosion in the leisurewear market, though by then Perry and Wegner had sold their financial interest to a raincoat supplier called Charles Mackintosh, finding that the internal running of the business had become onerous.

Perry signed an agreement to continue promoting the clothing wherever he travelled, a role he maintained when the company was later sold on again to the Figgie Corporation of Cleveland, Ohio. From then until almost the end of his life he was able to act as ambassador for the brand, making the occasional TV advertisement or opening stores in a variety of locations. Again this was a convenient arrangement, allowing Perry to indulge his love of travel while at the same time maintaining a link with his most successful commercial initiative.

Not all of Perry's ventures in this period had such happy outcomes. He did not enjoy, for example, his rare attempts to get involved in elite-level coaching. While happy to work with novice youngsters or wealthy beginners playing while on holiday, he lacked the patience and commitment necessary to work with top players. In a sign that he was not entirely *persona non grata* with the establishment in his homeland, the LTA invited him to liaise with the British Davis Cup team. He claimed afterwards that his role was not clear and his involvement was short-lived.

To an extent, Perry must take some of the blame for the slow pace of the thaw in his relationship with the British authorities. At a time when his popularity with the public and his visibility remained high in Britain – above all through broadcasting and business – after all that had gone before, the events of the 1930s still rankled. He admitted that he 'deliberately resisted' too much involvement in high-performance coaching schemes such as Davis Cup preparation, partly because it didn't necessarily suit his busy schedule but also it seems because he was not yet entirely willing to forget and forgive.

Even so, by the time he celebrated his 50th birthday in 1959, Perry's life had a more settled look than for many years past. Much of the reason for this was a fourth marriage that brought great happiness. Barbara (Bobby) Riese was the daughter of a Surrey stockbroker, and some ten years younger than Fred. She was divorced from her American husband and the couple first met in London, Perry in town commentating on Wimbledon and Bobby visiting her elderly mother. The pair married in 1953 and their daughter Penny was born in Florida five years later; Fred also adopted Bobby's son from her first marriage, David.

Although Perry's bronzed features and mid-Atlantic accent continued to attract female followers, this union, unlike his earlier ones, was enduring and hugely successful. Bunny Austin reflected when he met up again with his old friend in Florida that he noticed a big change in Perry over the years, 'He had married an enchanting wife... She was as fond of Fred as Fred was of her and of their daughter, Penny.'[11]

With both his domestic and working lives on an even keel, it remained to be seen whether the long-standing rift that lingered between Perry and his detractors in British tennis might finally be healed.

Conclusion: the tennis legend

A S HE entered his twilight years, Fred Perry continued to combine the teaching of tennis, commentating, business, and extensive travel. He remained an instantly recognisable figure in many parts of the world, his face and voice known particularly through his media work and his sportswear company.

Always on the lookout for new projects, Perry began the 1960s by working with an old friend to help set up a hotel in Jamaica, where he was appointed as director of golf. The deal was that his family could spend the winter months as guests at the Runaway Bay hotel while Fred was in charge of the golfing set-up. For more than 20 happy years Jamaica became a winter base, with many friends and celebrity names coming to visit and play a round or two on the plush course. His wife Bobby was a perfect companion in this latest initiative, for as Perry wrote in his memoirs she was a natural at 'the entertaining end' of proceedings and liked to travel; ideal, he added, as he had more-or-less 'lived out of a suitcase since 1930'.[1]

As well as residing for much of the year in Florida, the couple also purchased a property in England, at Rottingdean on the coast in Sussex, giving Fred a base when he came to Europe to watch and commentate at Wimbledon and other tournaments.

Perhaps the biggest change that came about in his later years – one that meant a huge amount to him – was a gradual improvement in Perry's fractured relationship with the British tennis establishment. Relations with the LTA and the All England Club were still frosty, as we saw, when Fred visited Britain for the first time in a decade during 1947. His honorary membership of the AEC, rescinded immediately when he turned professional, was restored in 1949, though this was not necessarily indicative of a full-scale mending of fences. At the time it avoided the embarrassment for Wimbledon of having a former champion on the premises commentating on the radio every year without being formally recognised. For much of the 1950s the LTA remained, in the view of tennis historian Robert Lake, 'riddled with southern-centric, patriarchal and elitist ideologies'.[2]

For as long as the tennis authorities continued to defend amateur traditions against Kramer-inspired professionalism, it was difficult for them to embrace Perry with any enthusiasm. The best that could be managed thus far was the presentation in 1959 of a silver cigarette box with the engraving 'F. J. Perry: From the Lawn Tennis Association and the All England Lawn Tennis Club to celebrate the 25th anniversary of your first Wimbledon'.

It was to take another decade still, by which time Fred was in his 60s, before the process of reconciliation sped up and became more apparent to the outside world. In part this was due simply to the passage of time. Most of the senior officials with whom Perry clashed had long since departed from prominent roles. Fred too had changed: no longer the youthful firebrand with rough edges, but more the dapper, relaxed, urbane media commentator.

Another crucial factor explaining why relationships between Perry and his erstwhile detractors improved immeasurably during the 1960s was that tennis was moving towards becoming 'open'. Having resisted change for many years, the ILTF reached landmark decisions in 1968, and within a few years distinctions between amateurs and professionals became a thing of the past. At long last, top players were entitled to be paid above board for their endeavours, and by the 1970s the sport was becoming – with official backing – a multi-million dollar enterprise.[3]

Perry was delighted that, despite hardline opposition in the past, reformers at both the All England Club and the LTA helped to push global opinion towards open tennis. By the late 1950s the AEC, concerned that Wimbledon would lose prestige if top amateurs continued to depart in ever larger numbers to join the pro ranks, was revising its stance. A key role in the process was played by AEC chairman Herman David – one of Fred's opponents on court in the 1930s – who publicly denounced amateurism as a 'living lie'. For Perry, this was a belated but resounding vindication of his decision to turn pro over 30 years earlier. Far from being a perpetual outsider, the path was finally clear for him to be warmly welcomed wherever he went in the tennis world. He was, in the words of the renowned journalist Richard Evans, a 'pariah turned patriarch'.[4]

There was one further, compelling reason why Perry was increasingly embraced by the same bodies who once shunned him. With each year that passed after 1945, and with no British man to emulate his success, particularly at Wimbledon, so Fred's status was magnified. He became more, in other words, than simply a patriarch or genial elder statesman: he was a living tennis legend. For the LTA and the AEC, it was a source of ever growing anxiety that Britain could not produce 'another Fred Perry'.

Whereas occasional Wimbledon victories in the 1960s and 1970s for women such as Angela Mortimer and Virginia Wade were proudly celebrated, no such success was forthcoming on the men's side, despite the media building up one hopeful after another as the most likely contender since the 1930s. With every year that passed, the scale of Fred's achievements became more obvious, and the desire to emulate such success more desperate. As well as eight victories in grand slam events, plus numerous other singles titles, he had a distinguished and enviable record in doubles – a total of 14 major titles in seven years. In the Davis Cup he had won 45 of 52 matches spread across 20 ties.

Of the generation of British men coming to the fore during and after the 1960s, Mark Cox won eight singles titles, Roger Taylor six and John Lloyd one – none of them in grand slam events and all in careers at least twice as long as Perry's. Among the cohort that followed, Greg Rusedski secured 15 titles (losing in one grand slam final) and Tim Henman 11 (without reaching a grand slam final). It was small wonder that in an opinion poll based on responses of 1,000 spectators queuing at Wimbledon for the 1984 Championships – before the arrival on the scene of Rusedski and Henman – 86 per cent nominated Perry as the British man who achieved most in world tennis in the previous 50 years.[5]

In a 2007 ranking exercise (before Andy Murray's career really blossomed), based on results in major tournaments and published in the tennis magazine *Ace*, Perry came out as the top British player since the First World War by a wide margin, with Bunny Austin second and Tim Henman third.[6]

In terms of the statistical record alone, the only possible rival to Perry for the title of Britain's most successful player prior to the emergence of Murray was Laurie

Doherty, who won the singles at Wimbledon five times and the doubles eight times, as well as remaining undefeated in Davis Cup ties. Doherty, however, performed under pre-1914 rules whereby the Wimbledon title-holder was only exposed to competition in the final round.

Perry had to contend with a far greater variety and depth of opposition in the 1930s: in the Davis Cup, and also in individual events, where he was confronted by high-calibre performers such as Australians Crawford and Quist; the Americans Vines, Wood, Allison and Budge; French musketeers such as Cochet and Borotra; plus the likes of Bunny Austin and von Cramm, two of the best players never to win Wimbledon.

As a result, Perry's name appears much more frequently than Doherty's on lists of all-time tennis greats. Perry's place among the best-of-the-best has been testified to in various quarters, for example by those who were his fiercest rivals in his prime playing days. Whether or not he eased back in their professional encounters, Elly Vines had the highest regard for his friend and business partner's ability on court. 'Perry had no weaknesses,' Vines reflected. 'He was a peerless net player and half-volleyer, his overhead was deadly, and … his forehand is best described as the finest Continental stroke in tennis history.'[7]

A similar assessment was made by Don Budge, who emphasised the importance of the Englishman's physicality on court. Only Tilden, Budge felt, could match Perry on this score. And then of course there was the Perry forehand, 'He could do so much with the shot, change direction on it so quickly and deceptively' – hence the lack of time for his opponent to prepare. Budge admitted that much of his own game was based on the way Perry played. As Duncan Macaulay noted, Budge, in taking over the mantle of the top amateur in the late 1930s, more than anything else derived from Perry a 'mentality of sustained aggression'.[8]

Among the top amateurs who came to the fore after the Second World War, Perry was held in similarly high regard. Ted Tinling noted that Fred's name came up in a conversation that took place in 1953 at a hotel in Australia during a Davis Cup tie. The home team was playing the United States, and several Wimbledon champions were present. It was agreed as the discussion turned to weighing up the best performers in the game since the Great War that Wimbledon would be the basis for assessment 'as it was the goal of every player'.

The consensus, Tinling recorded, was that four players, Tilden, Cochet, Perry and Budge, were 'unquestionably the elite of the game *to that time*'. Tinling was certain in his own mind that Perry's place in this group was fully deserved, especially as he had to vie with so many other skilful players in the 1930s. Despite this, his winning mentality ensured he lost only a couple of significant encounters in the entire period of his domination of amateur tennis from 1933 until the end of 1936. Adopting a longer perspective, taking into account the early part of the post-1968 open era, Tinling said he always firmly believed Perry 'was the greatest all-round player until Laver forced me to update my assessment'.[9]

Not all experts placed Perry quite so high. Lists of 'Great Players of All Time' compiled by the renowned tennis journalists Allison Danzig and Lance Tingay in the 1970s put Tilden at number one and either Budge or Laver as number two. Both Danzig and Tingay ranked Perry in sixth place, putting him in the most distinguished of company while not regarding him as among the very best. For Danzig there was almost nothing between the Englishman and his choice for fifth slot, Jack Kramer, 'Both were sterling competitors and splendid athletes, as well as superbly equipped in strokes.'[10]

Confirmation of the continuing regard for Perry's status arrived when he became the first non-American-born player to be inducted into the prestigious Tennis Hall of Fame in Newport, Rhode Island, in 1975. The International Hall of Fame, as it was known from that time on, used a glowing tribute to sum up Perry's game, 'None of his strokes was overpowering, but his attack was impetuous and relentless, ever challenging, and he ran like a deer in retrieving.'

Even as tennis moved into the more muscular era of Connors, McEnroe and Borg in the 1980s (after which it becomes difficult to make meaningful comparisons, given the huge changes in the speed and physicality of the modern sport), Perry's name still cropped up frequently as among the all-time legends. While acknowledging he was a friend for half a century, Dan Maskell in his autobiography ranked Perry at fourth, behind only Laver, Budge and Tilden. Maskell conceded there was far greater power and strength in depth in men's tennis by the 1980s, but he noted that technology and the regulations often favoured the modern player, for example allowing them to jump over (providing they did not touch) the service line, giving extra speed and bite to serving that was not possible in the 1930s.

Maskell based his judgement on criteria such as number of losses to inferior players and the ability to dominate by force of personality as much as by technical and physical attributes – an area in which he believed Perry was second to none. More surprisingly, given the acerbity of some of his other observations about Perry, Jack Kramer in his 1984 memoirs gave Fred the accolade of being the only non-American in his six players of the 'top rank'.[11]

As for his own views, for which he was frequently asked in later life, Perry was insistent – like many others – that Bill Tilden was peerless. Although he only encountered Tilden when he was past his prime, Perry commented in 1969 that the great American was remarkable even late in his career for never playing the same way twice, being able to mix up all sorts of styles and approaches. In his autobiography Fred was reluctant to compare himself with the generation of Borg and McEnroe (the latter an 'undoubted genius'), but he did describe Rod Laver as the most complete performer he watched after the war, a fiery competitor, with several heavy weapons such as his volley and awkward left-hand serve.

With a degree of self-effacement he often lacked in his pomp, Perry also acknowledged that whenever 'best-ever' lists were compiled, it probably helped his cause that he was forced to stop competing seriously after he shattered his elbow in 1941. One result of this was that photographs and recollections of him were often confined to the period in which he was at his peak. Some perhaps imagined him as 'a little better than I really was', he wrote, though it was accurate to say he never had qualms about refusing to give any quarter or to take prisoners on court.[12]

Perry's undisputed reputation as a tennis great was such that the All England Club decided to mark the 50th anniversary of his first Wimbledon triumph with special celebrations. With the smoke of past battles long gone, it was time on all sides to let bygones be bygones, though Fred almost never lived to enjoy the moment. He suffered a heart attack in 1983, and survived mainly because he was lucky enough to be in hospital being treated for another condition at the time the attack took place.

In May 1984, however, he was sufficiently well rested and recovered to enjoy a series of celebratory events, timed to coincide with his 75th birthday. The tributes began with the unveiling by the Duke of Kent, president of the AEC, of a statue of Perry, located on the concourse near to Centre Court and a familiar landmark to all subsequent visitors to Wimbledon. The three-quarter-life-size statue, specially commissioned by the renowned sculptor, David Wynne, showed Perry as he was in his 1930s heyday, smartly attired and hitting his famous forehand drive.

The nearby gates on Somerset Road were also named in his honour, 'The Fred Perry Gates'; the first time the AEC had made such a gesture since the days of the Doherty brothers. The marking of Fred's achievements continued at the Championships in July 1984 with what David Miller of *The Times* called a party 'the like of which not even Wimbledon has seen before'.

Among the 300 or so guests of Perry and his wife Bobby were long-standing friends such as Dan Maskell, golfer Henry Cotton and cricketer Denis Compton, filling the members' enclosure for a dinner dance which Miller wrote had some of 'the glister which the boisterous Fred once so enjoyed in Hollywood'.[13]

Perry was hugely touched. Of the statue and the naming of the gates he said in an interview afterwards, pointing back to the struggles of earlier years, 'It's a bit of an honour, isn't it, for an "ee-bah-goom" lad from the north.' Although his memoirs gave full vent to his anger about 'the shabby way' he felt he was treated in 1934, he ended his book on a mellower note. The chairman of the AEC, R.E.H. (Buzzer) Hadingham, commented publicly that he hoped Fred knew that in contrast to the social unfriendliness of earlier times, Wimbledon was 'today the most hospitable of clubs'.[14]

For several more years after 1984, Perry remained healthy enough to continue with an itinerant but enjoyable lifestyle. His typical annual calendar would find him travelling to all parts of the world: to Wimbledon and other grand slam events for commentating duties; undertaking children's teaching clinics in America; relaxing in Jamaica or at his attractive apartment in Boca West, Florida; and making occasional appearances on behalf of Fred Perry Sportswear (he remained in charge of the 'bullshit department', he said). When the original founder and name of the company turned up to open a store it was sometimes not the reception he expected, 'People are a little surprised that I'm still alive and breathing.'[15]

One of his most rewarding undertakings in his final years was being nominated by the International Tennis Federation to award, in conjunction with Don Budge and Lew Hoad, the annual title of men's world champion, an activity that took him back regularly to the scene of his first major triumph in 1933, New York. Meeting for a Masters series event each January, the three old warriors would reminisce while also deliberating on their choice of top player for the previous year.

For a man who had spent so much of his time on the road, it was fitting that Fred's last overseas trip, at the age of 85, took him to Australia, where early in 1934 he had followed up victory at Forest Hills the previous autumn with a second major title. In Melbourne to undertake commentary work at the Australian Open, he fell and cracked his ribs. He was released from hospital but after attending an Australian Hall of Fame dinner – 'tailored and dignified as ever', one of those present observed – the pain returned and he was readmitted.[16]

With his wife at his bedside, urged by doctors to continue talking to him so he relaxed in his last moments, he died on 2 February 1995. Perry had once told an interviewer that he was not a religious man. 'I take it as it comes. I assume that there is something beyond my ken, you might say, but I don't worry about it. I have to stick to tennis because it is all that I am mixed up in.'[17]

* * *

Fred Perry had lived a good life 'mixed up in' lawn tennis. His funeral took place on a rainy day a few weeks later at Rottingdean in Sussex, and in June 1995 – just ahead of the start of the Championships – a memorial service attended by the great and the good of the tennis world, including several Wimbledon champions, was held at St Paul's Cathedral in London. Some of the warmest tributes in this period of reflection were made, appropriately enough, by American friends and former playing rivals.

George Lott, who observed Perry close up in their days on the pro tour in the late 1930s, summed up his playing ability, describing him as someone who 'not only possessed but also exhibited the qualities so necessary in a champion, namely confidence, concentration, condition, co-ordination, courage and fortitude, determination, stamina, quickness and speed'. Lott even likened Perry to renowned American sporting greats, observing lyrically that he had 'the swashbuckling good looks and supreme confidence of a Walter Hagen; the grace and ease of a Joe DiMaggio gathering in a fly ball... the skill and know-how of a Tilden'. The main address at the St Paul's memorial service was also given by an American, 1955 Wimbledon champion Tony Trabert, who spoke more prosaically about Perry the man: charming, engaging, often mischievous; for the most part 'simply fun to be around'.[18]

Yet despite all that the United States had offered to and meant to Perry, from his earliest breakthrough days in tennis to the end of his life, he still hankered after his homeland. At his funeral his daughter Penny commented that, though he chose to become a US citizen and spent so much of his time on the road, he felt that he ultimately belonged in England. It seems clear that the 1984 celebrations at Wimbledon marked the moment in his mind when he at last secured the recognition from the British tennis establishment that he long craved.

It was no coincidence that the final sentences of his memoirs noted how he was more proud than he could say of the unveiling of the statue in the grounds of the AEC and the naming of the Fred Perry Gates in Somerset

Road. 'The occasion', he wrote tellingly, 'meant more to me than all the prize money in the world.'

After 1984 Fred was often seen during the Wimbledon fortnight standing on the concourse outside Centre Court, posing for photographs with fans, and after his cremation in 1995 his ashes were taken to SW19 to be placed in the grounds of the All England Club beneath the statue.[19]

It had not always been the case, but in his last years Fred Perry was – fully, finally and without equivocation – 'a popular champion at home'.

Notes

Introduction, 'Perry is not a popular champion at home'

1   Jack Kramer (with Frank Deford), *The Game – My 40 Years in Tennis* (London, 1981), pp. 19-20. For the themes in this introduction, see Kevin Jefferys 'Fred Perry and British Tennis: "Fifty Years to Honor a Winner"', *Sport in History*, 29, 1 (2009), pp. 1-24.

2   F.R. Burrow, *The Centre Court and Others* (London, 1937), p. 192.

3   Ted Tinling, *Tinling: Sixty Years in Tennis* (London, 1983), p. 196.

4   *The Times*, 7 July 1934; *Lawn Tennis and Badminton*, 14 July 1934.

5   *Lawn Tennis and Badminton*, 14 July 1934.

6   Fred Perry, *Fred Perry: An Autobiography* (London, 1984), pp. 10-11.

7   Robert Winder, *Half-Time. The Glorious Summer of 1934* (London, 2016 edn), pp. 170-9, notes that Perry's autobiography refers, for example, to him winning the mixed doubles with Miss Round at Wimbledon in 1934, when in fact this occurred in 1935 and 1936.

8   Perry, *Autobiography*, p. 78.

9   *The Times*, 23 May 1984; Jon Henderson, *Best of British. Hendo's Sporting Heroes* (London, 2007).

10   Jon Henderson, *The Last Champion. The Life of Fred Perry* (London, 2009).

11 e.g. Mark Hodgkinson, *Andy Murray Wimbledon Champion: The Full and Extraordinary Story* (London, 2013); Andy Murray, *Seventy-Seven: My Road to Wimbledon Glory* (London, 2013).

12 Perry, *Autobiography*, p. 111.

13 John Roberts, *The Independent*, 3 February 1995; Reg Lansberry, 'Fifty Years to Honor a Winner', *World Tennis*, July 1984, p. 73.

1 Moving from north to south

1 Perry, *Autobiography*, p. 9; 'Perry: World's Finest Tennis Amateur Banks Heavily on Luck', *Newsweek*, 7 September 1935.

2 Friedrich Engels, *The Condition of the Working Classes in England* (London, 1840), p. 212.

3 Keith Gildart, 'Samuel Frederick Perry', in Gildart and David Howell (eds), *Dictionary of Labour Biography*, Vol XII (London and Basingstoke, 2005), pp. 226-33.

4 Greg Rosen, *Serving the People. Co-operative Party History from Fred Perry to Gordon Brown* (London, 2007), p. 2.

5 Perry, *Autobiography*, p. 15.

6 *The LTA Annual Handbook, 1922* (London, 1922): Lancashire had 61 clubs affiliated to the LTA and Cheshire 45, compared with 129 found in Middlesex.

7 Perry, *Autobiography*, pp. 15-16; 'Perry of Ealing' interview in *Ealing Gazette*, 6 July 1984; Stan Hart, *Once a Champion. Legendary Tennis Stars Revisited* (New York, 1985, p. 75.

8 Fred Perry, *My Story* (London, 1934) pp. 273-4.

9 Henderson, *Last Champion*, pp. 26-33.

10 Perry, *Autobiography*, pp. 25-6; Gildart, 'Samuel Frederick Perry', *Dictionary of Labour Biography*.

11 Henry Wancke, 'Interview: Fred Perry', *Tennis World*, August 1986, pp. 49-51.

12 John Parsons, *The Ultimate Encyclopedia of Tennis: The Definitive Illustrated Guide to World Tennis* (London, 1998), p. 95; Perry, *Autobiography*, p. 19.

2 Entering the world of elite tennis

1 Frank Deford, *Big Bill Tilden: The Triumphs and the Tragedy* (Delaware, 2004 edn), pp. 11-24.

2 Ted Tinling, *Love and Faults: Personalities who have Changed the History of Tennis in my Lifetime* (New York, 1979), p. 144. See also Kevin Jefferys, 'The Heyday of Amateurism in Modern Lawn Tennis', *International Journal of the History of Sport*, 26, 15 (2009), pp. 2236-52.

3 Alan Little, *Wimbledon 1922-2002. The Changing Face of Church Road* (Wimbledon, 2002), p. 2.

4 Cited in Mike Huggins and Jack Williams, *Sport and the English 1918-39* (Abingdon, 2006), p. 99.

5 Max Robertson (ed), *The Encyclopedia of Tennis* (London, 1974), p. 90.

6 David Allaby, *Wimbledon of the North. 100 Years at the Northern* (Didsbury, 1981), pp. 33-4 and 58. See also the biography of Woosnam by Mick Collins, *All-Round Genius* (London, 2006).

7 Tinling, *Sixty Years in Tennis*, p. 193.

8 E. Digby Baltzell, *Sporting Gentlemen: Men's Tennis from the Age of Honor to the Cult of the Superstar* (New York, 1995), pp. 189 and 221.

9 Winder, *Half-Time*, p. 5. Perry's reference to his lower middle-class status comes from a British Pathe interview, July 1970.

10 Dan Maskell, *Oh I Say!* (London, 1989), pp. 78 and 109. See also Robert J. Lake, '"That Excellent Sample of a Professional": Dan Maskell and the Contradictions of British Amateurism in Twentieth-Century Lawn Tennis', *Sport in History*, 36, 1 (2016), pp. 1-25.

11 Huw D. Evans, *Ted Avory. A Life in Tennis* (Wimbledon, 1995), pp. 7-13.

12 H.W. Austin & Phyllis Konstam, *A Mixed Double* (London, 1969), pp. 229-30.

13 G.P. Hughes, *British Lawn Tennis*, March 1947, p. 4; Tinling, *Sixty Years in Tennis*, p. 193.

14 Tinling, *Sixty Years in Tennis*, p. 193; Perry, *Autobiography*, p. 18.

15 Perry, *My Story*, pp. 20-1; Perry, *Autobiography*, pp. 34-5; Lansberry, 'Fifty Years to Honor a Winner', *World Tennis*, 1984, p. 73.

16 Burrow, *The Centre Court*, p. 158.

3 On the rise

1 *New York Times* obituary, 3 February 1995.

2 G.P. Hughes, *Improving Your Tennis* (London, 1947), pp. 21-2; Perry, *Autobiography*, p. 24.

3 Perry in Max Robertson (ed), *The LTA Book of the Game* (London, 1957), pp. 18-21.

4 Norah Cleather, *Wimbledon Story* (London, 1947), p. 103.

5 Tinling, *Sixty Years in Tennis*, p. 194; Maskell, *Oh I Say!*, p. 145.

6 Perry, *My Story*, dedication page and pp. 278-9.

7 Perry, *Autobiography*, p. 23; Perry, *My Story*, p. 21.

8 Ellsworth Vines III, *The Greatest Athlete of All Time* (Bloomington, 1985), pp. 4-7; Perry, *My Story*, pp. 25-6.

9 Tinling, *Love and Faults*, p. 144; Perry, *Autobiography*, p. 44.

4 Davis Cup drama

1 Tinling, *Love and Faults*, p. 144.

2 Perry, *My Story*, pp. 29-31.

3 Tinling, *Sixty Years in Tennis*, p. 194.

4 Maskell, *Oh I Say!*, p. 155; Perry, *My Story*, p. 32.

5 Herbert Warren Wind, 'The Sporting Scene. An Old Cab Horse and Two New Ones', *New Yorker* magazine, 21 October 1985, p. 81.

6 Burrow, *The Centre Court*, pp. 169-70.

7 Cited in Henderson, *Last Champion*, p. 71.

8 Arthur Wallis Myers, *Great Lawn Tennis* (London, 1937), p. 134.

9 Bellamy, in Ronald Atkin (ed), *For the Love of Tennis* (London, 1985), p. 157.

10 Perry, *Autobiography*, p. 39; Perry, *My Story*, pp. 46-7.

11 Vines, *Greatest Athlete*, p. 40; Perry, *My Story*, pp. 49-53.

12 Perry, *Autobiography*, pp. 42-5.

13 Perry, *Autobiography*, p. 43.

5 A year of disappointments

1 *The Times*, 3 June 1932.

2 Duncan Macaulay, *Behind the Scenes at Wimbledon* (London, 1965), p. 74.

3 Perry, *My Story*, p. 286.

4 Perry, *My Story*, p. 59.

5 Perry, *Autobiography*, p. 49. Trengrove, *Story of the Davis Cup*, p. 112 writes that the only public protest of note about Prenn's treatment came in a letter to *The Times*, signed by Austin and Perry, expressing 'great misgivings' at any action which undermined the role of sport as a promoter of international understanding and a human activity that should contain no distinctions of race, class or creed.

6 Perry, *My Story*, pp. 60-1.

7 Evans, *Ted Avory*, p. 14.

8 Perry, *My Story*, p. 288.

9 Evans, *Ted Avory*, p. 15.

6 Triumph in Paris

1 Maskell, *Oh I Say!*, pp. 151-4.

2 This episode was recalled in *The Times*, 11 January 1972.

3 *Daily Telegraph*, 4 June 1933.

4 Burrow, *The Centre Court*, pp. 181-2.

5 Maskell, *Oh I Say!*, pp. 162-5; E.C. Potter, *The Davis Cup* (London, 1969), p. 79.

6 Perry, *Autobiography*, pp. 61-3; *Daily Telegraph*, 28 July 1933.

7 Perry, *My Story*, p. 86; Perry, *Autobiography*, p. 65.

8 Maskell, *Oh I Say!*, pp. 175-6; Austin, *A Mixed Double*, pp. 72-9.

9 *Daily Telegraph*, 31 July 1933.

7 American and Australian champion

1 Perry, *Autobiography*, p. 66.

2 Vines and Vier, *Myth and Method*, p. 11; Vines, *Greatest Athlete*, p. 369.

3 Rex Bellamy, *The Tennis Set* (London, 1972), p. 183.

4 Perry, *My Story*, p. 98.

5 Perry, *Autobiography*, p. 68; Perry, *My Story*, p. 99.

6 Perry, *Autobiography*, pp. 70-3.

7 *The Times*, 26-27 January 1934.

8 Cited in Henderson, *Last Champion*, p. 125.

9 'Perry: World's Finest Tennis Amateur', *Newsweek*, 7 September 1935 claims that the previous winter the American promoter Bill O'Brien offered him $50,000 to turn professional.

10 Jefferys, 'Heyday of Amateurism', *International Journal of the History of Sport*, (2009), p. 2247.

11 Perry, *My Story*, pp. 150-3; Perry, *Autobiography*, p. 74 (italics are those used by Perry).

12 *Lawn Tennis and Badminton*, 31 March 1934.

8 World number one

1 *The Times*, 30 May 1934.

2 Burrow, *The Centre Court*, p. 192.

3 Perry, *Autobiography*, pp. 11 and 78-9. In *Half-Time*, Robert Winder suggests (pp. 177-8) that the 1984 story of Perry being insulted in the dressing rooms may be 'a notch too good to be true', noting that Perry makes no mention of it when writing about the final in 1936. But the additional updating material in the 1936 book *Perry on Tennis* (mostly an abridged version of Perry's 1934 *My Story*) was penned in the immediate aftermath of the 1936 Wimbledon final. Fred was about to play in another Davis Cup final and planned to play in the US Championships as well; his real venom towards the LTA understandably came *after* he had finally quit the amateur ranks, when he was keen to justify and defend his actions with as much evidence as possible. Prior to him turning pro his views on the whole topic of paid play, though detectable from reading between the lines of his writings, were always expressed in a balanced way.

4 Henderson, *Last Champion*, pp. 141 and 153.

5 Robertson (ed), *Encyclopedia of Tennis*, p. 189. See also Henderson, *Last Champion*, p. 155.

6 Mike Huggins, 'BBC Radio and Sport 1922-39', *Contemporary British History*, 21, 4 (2007), pp. 494-511.

7 Tinling, *Love and Faults*, p. 147; Tinling, *Sixty Years in Tennis*, pp. 167 and 196-7.

8 *Lawn Tennis and Badminton*, 14 July 1934.

9 Perry, *Autobiography*, p. 83.

10 William X. Shields, *Bigger than Life. A Biography of Francis X. Shields* (New York, 1986), pp. xviii, 51 and 79.

11 Tinling, *Love and Faults*, p. 143; Trengrove, *Story of the Davis Cup*, p. 116.

12 'Perry: World's Finest Tennis Amateur', *Newsweek*, 7 September 1935.

9 On the brink

1 *The Times*, 12 January 1935.

2 Perry, *Autobiography*, p. 87.

3 Fred J. Perry, *Perry on Tennis: Expert Advice for All on Lawn Tennis* (London, 1936), pp. 85-9.

4 *The Times*, 1-5 June 1935.

5 Burrow, *The Centre Court*, pp. 201-2; Macaulay, *Behind the Scenes at Wimbledon*, pp. 104-6.

6 Perry, 'What's Wrong with American Tennis', *Collier's*, 30 March 1935; Trengrove, *Story of the Davis Cup*, p. 121.

7 Perry, *Autobiography*, pp. 93-4. Perry was more restrained in his 1936 account, penned closer to the events described, when he wrote that having 'dished it out' to opponents, it was his turn to 'take it', adding that he did not begrudge Allison his victory: *Perry on Tennis*, pp. 94-5.

8 John Olliff, *The Romance of Wimbledon* (London, 1949), p. 105; Perry, *Autobiography*, p. 94.

9 Perry, *Autobiography*, p. 95.

10 Swapping 'glory for gold'

1 Perry, *Autobiography*, p. 96.

2 J.A. Cross, *Sir Samuel Hoare* (London, 1977), p. 351; Sir Samuel Hoare, *The Unbroken Thread* (London, 1949), p. 197. Hoare's 1954 account of his public life in the 1930s, *Nine Troubled Years*, makes no reference to his spell as president of the LTA.

3 *The Times*, 30 May-2 June 1936.

4 Perry, *Autobiography*, pp. 97-8.

5 Macaulay, *Behind the Scenes at Wimbledon*, p. 115.

6 *Tennis Illustrated*, July 1936, p. 14.

7 Tinling, *Sixty Years in Tennis*, p. 196.

8 Maskell, *Oh I Say!*, pp. 178-9.

9 Wallis Myers, *Great Lawn Tennis*, pp. 205-7.

10 Kramer, *The Game*, pp. 60-1.

11 *Manchester Guardian*, 10 November 1936; Maskell, *Oh I Say!*, p. 179.

12 *Lawn Tennis and Badminton*, 5 and 19 December 1936.

13 Wancke, 'Interview: Fred Perry', *Tennis World*, August 1986, pp. 49-51. Perry, *Autobiography*, pp. 108-9.

14 Evans, *Ted Avory*, p. 14.

15 Perry, *Autobiography*, p. 110.

16 Jefferys, 'Heyday of Amateurism', *International Journal of the History of Sport*, p. 2250.

17 Budge, *Budge on Tennis*, pp. 15-17.

18 Perry, *Autobiography*, p. 108.

11 Life on the pro tour

1 George Lott, 'Inside Tennis', *Atlantic Monthly*, January 1938, pp. 77-81.

2   Lott, 'Inside Tennis', *Atlantic Monthly*, January 1938; Perry, *Autobiography*, p. 120.

3 Perry, *Autobiography*, p. 118; Herbert Warren Wind, 'The Sporting Scene', *New Yorker* magazine, 21 October 1985, p. 62; Robert J. Lake, *A Social History of Tennis in Britain* (Abingdon, 2014), pp. 192-4

4 Vines, *Greatest Athlete*, p. 138.

5 Perry, *Autobiography*, pp. 111-16.

6 Lott, 'Inside Tennis', *Atlantic Monthly*, January 1938.

7 Perry, *Autobiography*, pp. 121-2

8 Vines, *Greatest Athlete*, p. 138; *Sunday Times*, 5 February 1985. See also Stan Hart, *Once a Champion*, p. 231.

9 Maskell, *Oh I Say!*, p. 179.

10 Joe McCauley, *The History of Professional Tennis* (Windsor, 2000), p. 32.

11 Perry, *Autobiography*, p. 132; Henderson, *Last Champion*, pp. 229-31; Winder, *Half-Time*, pp. 219-20.

12 McCauley, *History of Professional Tennis*, pp. 34-5.

12 Coach, commentator, businessman

1 Perry, *Autobiography*, pp. 134-6; Trengrove, *Story of the Davis Cup*, p. 144.

2 Perry, *Autobiography*, pp. 137-8; McCauley, *History of Professional Tennis*, p. 41; Herbert Warren Wind, 'The Sporting Scene', *New Yorker* magazine, 21 October 1985, p. 90.

3 Norman Cutler, *Inside Tennis* (London, 1954), pp. 16-19.

4 Tinling, *Sixty Years in Tennis*, p. 197.

5 Perry, *Autobiography*, p. 140. Sam Perry was to die in 1954, though Fred was able to see him a few more times on his regular trips to England after 1947.

6 *Daily Telegraph* obituary, 3 February 1995; Perry, *Autobiography*, pp. 141 and 190.

7 Alan Mills, *Lifting the Covers. The Autobiography* (London, 2005), p. 68.

8 Maskell, *Oh I Say!*, p. 257; Perry, *Autobiography*, p. 141.

9 Perry, *Autobiography*, pp. 142-7.

10 Henderson, *Last Champion*, pp. 247-53; Perry, *Autobiography*, pp. 148-9.

11 Austin, *A Mixed Double*, p. 230.

Conclusion: the tennis legend

1 Perry, *Autobiography*, pp. 186 and 190; Stan Hart, *Once a Champion*, p. 67.

2 Lake, *Social History of Tennis*, p. 199.

3 Kevin Jefferys, 'The Triumph of Professionalism in World Tennis: The Road to 1968', *International Journal of the History of Sport*, 26, 15 (2009), pp. 2253-89.

4 *Sunday Times*, 5 February 1985.

5 Norman Giller (ed), *The Book of Tennis Lists* (London, 1985), p. 195.

6 John Haylett, 'Brits Who Ruled the Waves', *Ace* magazine, March 2007.

7 Vines, *Tennis. Myth and Method*, p. 11.

8 Macaulay, *Behind the Scenes at Wimbledon*, p. 121; Budge, *Budge on Tennis*, pp. 47, 61 and 121.

9 Tinling, *Love and Faults*, p. 142 (Tinling's italics).

10 Robertson (ed), *Encyclopedia of Tennis*, pp. 166-75.

11 Maskell, *Oh I Say!*, pp. 330-1; Kramer, *The Game*, pp. 44 and 295.

12 Perry, *Autobiography*, pp. 172-6; *The Times*, 8 July 1969.

13 *The Times*, 7 July 1984.

14 Interview with David Miller, *The Times*, 18 May 1984; John Roberts, *The Independent*, 3 February 1995.

15 Wancke, 'Interview: Fred Perry', *Tennis World*, August 1986, pp. 49-51.

16 Richard Evans, *Sunday Times*, 5 February 1985.

17 Hart, *Once a Champion*, pp. 73-5.

18 George Lott, cited in Richard Williams, 'The perfect stage for a class act', *Guardian*, 17 June 2004; Henderson, *Last Champion*, p. 282.

19 Perry, *Autobiography*, pp. 10 and 194-5; Henderson, *Last Champion*, pp. 281-2; Wancke, 'Interview: Fred Perry', *Tennis World*, August 1986, pp. 49-51.

Select Bibliography

Details of the range of materials upon which this biography is based, such as tennis journals and magazines, autobiographies and secondary works, are found in the Notes. Below are listed a few of the key books that help to illuminate Perry's career:

H.W. (Bunny) Austin & Phyllis Konstam, *A Mixed Double* (London: Chatto and Windus, 1969)

Frank Deford, *Big Bill Tilden: The Triumphs and the Tragedy* (Delaware: Sport Media Publishing, 2004 edn)

Huw D. Evans, *Ted Avory. A Life in Tennis* (London: All England Lawn Tennis Club, 1995)

Jon Henderson, *The Last Champion. The Life of Fred Perry* (London: Yellow Jersey Press, 2009)

Jack Kramer (with Frank Deford), *The Game – My 40 Years in Tennis* (London: Andre Deutsch, 1981)

Robert J. Lake, *A Social History of Tennis in Britain* (Abingdon: Routledge, 2014)

Alan Little, *Wimbledon 1922-2002. The Changing Face of Church Road* (Wimbledon: Lawn Tennis Museum, 2002)

Joe McCauley, *The History of Professional Tennis* (Windsor: Short Run Books, 2000)

Dan Maskell, *Oh I Say!* (London: Fontana, 1989)

Fred Perry, *My Story* (London: Hutchinson, 1934)

Fred Perry, *Fred Perry: An Autobiography* (London: Hutchinson, 1984)

Ted Tinling, *Tinling: Sixty Years in Tennis* (London: Sidgwick and Jackson, 1983)

Alan Trengrove, *The Story of the Davis Cup* (London: Stanley Paul, 1985)

Ellsworth Vines III, *The Greatest Athlete of All Time* (Bloomington USA: 1st Books, 1985)

Robert Winder, *Half-Time. The Glorious Summer of 1934* (London: Wisden & Co./Bloomsbury, 2016 edn)

Index